£2.50
Ge

17/41

KU-411-094

'The literary antidote to the poison of true-crime mags and serial-killer biographies . . . a strong, emotive, moral book'
– Stephen McGinty, *The Herald*

'A great work of narrative non-fiction. Both a memoir of childhood and a detective novel, a social history and a dissection of our craving for "true crime", it is impassioned and exhaustively researched, and one of the best books written from the margins of British society since Orwell's *Down and Out in Paris and London*'
– Tim Adams, *Elle*

'A fine book. On the one hand it is full of the innocent mysticism of childhood, which is always threatened by the knowledge that adulthood brings. On the other, it is an indictment of Britain in the late twentieth century – a once benign place turned hard and evil. It will remain with the reader long after the last page is finished'.
– Mark Timlin, *Time Out*

'O'Hagan's history is the history of many modern Glaswegians, but his account of it is peculiarly honest ... a remarkable book'

— Gavin Stamp, *Spectator*

'*The Missing* is an astonishingly powerful and successful book ... in its painstaking reclaiming of his victims' world, *The Missing* is haunting and deeply affecting'

— Dermot Bolger, *Irish Tribune*

'It is as though in the world of "mispers" (missing persons) he has found the true borderlands between fact and fiction, where no one is who they once were ... *The Missing* is a memorable book'

— Ian Bell, *Times Literary Supplement*

THE MISSING

Andrew O'Hagan read English at the University of Strathclyde, and was, for four years, an assistant editor of the *London Review of Books*. He is now on the paper's editorial board, and he writes for the *Guardian* and *Esquire*. *The Missing* is his first book.

Andrew O'Hagan

THE MISSING

PICADOR

First published 1995 by Picador

This edition published 1996 by Picador
an imprint of Macmillan Publishers Ltd
25 Eccleston Place, London SW1W 9NF
and Basingstoke

Associated companies throughout the world

ISBN 0 330 34137 5

Copyright © Andrew O'Hagan 1995

The right of Andrew O'Hagan to be identified as the
author of this work has been asserted by him in accordance
with the Copyright, Designs and Patents Act 1988.

Parts of this book were originally published in slightly
different form in the *London Review of Books*.

All rights reserved. No part of this publication may be
reproduced, stored in or introduced into a retrieval system,
or transmitted, in any form, or by any means (electronic, mechanical,
photocopying, recording or otherwise) without the prior written
permission of the publisher. Any person who does any unauthorized
act in relation to this publication may be liable to criminal
prosecution and civil claims for damages.

9 8 7 6 5 4 3 2 1

A CIP catalogue record for this book is available from
the British Library.

Phototypeset by Intype London Ltd
Printed by Mackays of Chatham PLC, Chatham, Kent

This book is sold subject to the condition that it shall not,
by way of trade or otherwise, be lent, re-sold, hired out,
or otherwise circulated without the publisher's prior consent
in any form of binding or cover other than that in which
it is published and without a similar condition including this
condition being imposed on the subsequent purchaser.

This book is dedicated to Nancy, my mother
and to the memory of my grandmothers
Agnes Kelly Dunn Docherty (1912–88)
Mary Lavery O'Hagan (1900–81)

'His soul had approached that region where dwell the vast hosts of the dead. He was conscious of, but could not apprehend, their wayward and flickering existence. His own identity was fading out into a grey impalpable world: the solid world itself which these dead had one time reared and lived in was dissolving and dwindling.'

James Joyce, *The Dead*

CONTENTS

Book One
THE CANDLEWICK

CLYDE-BUILT

IN THOSE DAYS, the town was brand new and the heaters smelt like nothing on earth. I was five, with my face up against the hot copper grill, sniffing the weird air as it drifted into the morning. They were mounted a few inches from the floor in every room, the white electric fires. I can hear their thermostatic click even now, and sometimes, walking in a strange room, some bland electrical hotness on my face brings them tingling back. It's the least important thing. When I think of them, especially the one in my mother's bedroom of twenty years ago, and I recall the purple candlewick that covered her bed opposite, something unfolds and spreads out in my head. A day opens up right in front of me, like it was never away.

The man from the Corporation was fixing the bin-cupboard by the front door; trying, I think, to rip out the hinges and put in new ones. He kept going on about Rangers and Celtic to a joiner working at the next house along. I could hear their voices from upstairs, where I sat by the fire chewing a corner of the candlewick. I stood up on bare feet, and walked to the boiler, a round thing wearing a furry jacket that hung in a built-in cupboard. They called it the immerser. I put my arms around it, and strained to make them go all the way, but even with my fingers at full stretch I couldn't grab the wooden thing behind. There was something there; I knew there was; it had been there for ages. My right hand could just flick the edge of the thing, just about pinch a corner, but there was no grabbing it. In the end I squeezed my body halfway round, and pulled hard until it loosened and fell into the middle of the room with me underneath.

I knew the face framed by that rickety wood. I'd seen it before, in that frame, and I knew who it was: my grandfather Michael. I knew that's who it was though I'd never met him. The grandfather was covered in dust and damp patches dried in. But that was him: he had the darkest eyes I'd ever seen. His hair was slick, combed up to a glistening ridge; the lips were thin, the cheeks white. It looked as if someone had gone round his ears with a pencil. My granda Michael looked like Glasgow: a place that felt far away by then, that sounded old and big and always in the dark. Just over twenty miles away from our coastal New Town of wall-heaters and bin-cupboards, it was the place where we were all born. Glasgow sounded like Granda to me; I was sure they were one and the same.

I sometimes went back to the picture, and I got to know a little more as time went by. He was missing. I'd never seen him, and I was born twenty-eight years after he disappeared at sea. I couldn't get over these bits of information. He looked like Glasgow. He was missing at sea. In another time, when I'd come to look something like the man in the picture, I looked at the photograph again, and noticed how my grandfather Michael hadn't changed a bit. He was missing, and was to be for ever dark-eyed, with a forehead fit to launch ships with.

HMS *FORFAR* WAS built by Fairfield, and launched, first as HMS *Montrose*, just before Christmas 1920. An armed merchant cruiser of the *Campbell* class, she was fitted with eight six-inch guns and two three-inch anti-aircraft batteries. In 1940, the ship was guarding the sea around the Shetland Isles and, sometimes, it would lead a convoy through the dangerous waters off the west of Ireland. A fair number of Scots manned the ship during the closing months of 1940: Ian Affleck, an engineer to trade, not far up in his twenties, used to work in Kalac's Cycle and Motor Store in Forfar, and felt he'd been born to help power a ship such as this, named after his own town. Angus McInnes's father had been a fisherman on the Isle of Harris and Angus had sailed with *Forfar* since early in the war, working as a lamp-trimmer. He was good pals with an assistant cook called James Wilson McGinlay, who was a bit younger. McGinlay's father was a coachman at Milton, in Glasgow, a fact which eventually brought James into nodding and tobacco-loaning relations with my grandfather, Michael O'Hagan, who came from Glasgow's Calton district. They say James was shy, though, and when people would ask him how come he had two second names he'd just blush, and mutter something about being quite lucky. Michael protected him, after his own style. My granda spent most time though with Jim Reilly, who was in most respects like himself, from the Calton, with a small but persistent history of personal trouble left behind him.

My grandmother Molly had worked in the family fish-monger's at Millroad Street for years. Jeannie and Katie, also in the family, gutted and cleaned beside her, with old Annie Lavery keeping a watchful eye. In time, Molly would take to attending Mass every morning; the rest of the time, according to Jeannie, was spent worrying about costs and cleanliness and relatives and boats. She'd say a decade for you as soon as look at you. There had been worries with Michael in the past; things might be easier when the war got finished. Their first boy had been born nearly ten years before my father Gerald, and was baptized over in St Mary's on 11 March 1928. His name was Gerard. A year later, after pulling a pot of boiling water down off the fire, the baby Gerard died at the Royal Infirmary from scalding and secondary shock. Michael signed the death certificate with a neat hand, and doubtless never forgot it. The first boy in his own family – his elder brother Hugh – had died exactly the same way in 1894, at the same age, in the scullery of his parents' house at 40 Candleriggs.

Some time, say in November 1940, my grandmother Molly received an undated letter from Liverpool, where *Forfar* was docked. It was the last contact she would ever have with her troubled young husband.

22a Woodstock Gardens
Liverpool

Dear Molly
This is the first time I had the opportunity to write. I couldn't send anything as I promised because I got into some trouble and got my pay stopped. I haven't had the price of smokes since I got back and I won't get any for a fortnight yet. Use

the above address and I will get an answer quicker it is a fellow on the ships address. I am glad you and the kids are not here the bombing is terrible. I hope the same thing never comes to Glasgow. Tell Annie, Jeannie, May, Katie and them all I was asking for them. I hope you and the kids are keeping well I will be here for some time yet. I will draw to a close sending you and the kids my best love.

Michael

At the crack of December 1940 conditions in the sea around Britain were hellish. In more peaceful times, many would reflect that this was the most dangerous period for British ships, on any stretch of water, since the Armada. But December might have proved better. Storms in the North Atlantic were hampering the success of German U-boats, who at this point in the war, under the command of Admiral Dönitz, were promising to obliterate the Royal Navy. Many on board *Forfar*, especially among the O'Neills and the O'Hagans, greatly resented the refusal of Eire to allow ships such as theirs to pull in at bases on the Irish coast. It left them crazily exposed to U-boat attack in the merciless waters of the western approaches. On 2 December, the weather was bad, and *Forfar* was escorting a convoy through this area, 15 degrees and 20 minutes west. The water stirred violently as the ships tried to point a steady course northward.

A thin strip of darkness, U-boat 99, commanded by the notorious Kretschmer, cut through the waters off Ireland soon after the last light had gone. It was soon joined by three other subs, part of the 'wolf-pack' strategy favoured by Dönitz, who also saw the advantage in having these boats travel towards the threatened convoy at night, and on the surface. The Royal Navy suffered greatly from this – they had been concentrating their efforts on the disabling of submerged boats, and hadn't expected group attacks in the dark, from near-invisible silhouettes floating on top of the water. As it turned out, thirty-seven British ships were lost in December, mostly the work of three U-boat aces: Kretschmer, Schepke (in U-100), and Prien (in U-47). Overall command came from Lorient, on the by now captured French coast. Information from German scout-planes on the location of enemy targets would be passed, by radio signal, to the commanders in charge of the hunting packs. One U-boat would shadow the convoy, and direct the other subs by wireless, until they were all able to home in at once.

The convoy headed by *Forfar*, HX90, having been much put out by the weather, was not expecting a late-night attack. A dozen men played cards along a disused bit of machinery, in a tight corridor off the kitchens, as *Forfar* cut ahead of the convoy at full speed. Michael was a greaser, and also a fireman, and he appears to have been away from the engine-room when the first torpedo struck. A giant shudder filled the ship, followed by a crack and the sound of steam escaping. Those on top could hear other torpedoes swish past, missing *Forfar*, some plunging into ships to the rear, others going nowhere. There was a panic, and a failure in lowering some lifeboats, and a burning of hands as the ropes unfurled at speed. Great shouts ripped through the dark – men running, going over the side, and many falling quiet where they'd sat. More torpedoes delved into the side. Lifeboats dropped into the oily water, lit now with bursts of flame. The noise was horrible, the smell unforgettable, as the rowers did their best to heave themselves clear of the burning vessels. By morning, eleven of the convoy's ships were sunk.

A telegram stamped 'priority' arrived at 9 Sydney Street exactly a week later. 'I deeply regret to inform you,' it said, 'that your husband Michael O'Hagan is reported missing on war service.' One or two of Molly's co-workers, gutting the fish with unusual quietness, had known of the ship's sinking before that day, and word had spread, but no one could face telling Molly or any of the women who had men on the boats. They left her pretty much alone with the telegram that day, but gathered round the day after, when a letter arrived from the naval registrar at Wood Street School in Cardiff.

Cardiff 8950   10 December 1940

Dear Madam

It is with very deep regret that I have to confirm my telegram telling you that your husband Michael Moran O'Hagan (Greaser) is reported to be missing and that he has probably lost his life on war service. Although it cannot yet be officially presumed that he is dead (in view of the faint possibility that he may have been picked up by another vessel), I can hold out very little hope that he is alive.

Please allow me, therefore, on behalf of the officers and men of the Royal and Merchant Navies, the high tradition of which your husband has helped to maintain, to express sincere sympathy with you in this anxious time.
Yours sincerely

EDGAR IRVINE
Registrar General

After *Forfar* was gone, anxiety came and went, and then went a bit more. As the months passed, and the news grew old, various accounts of the sinking were still exchanged over back-courts in the Calton. It was said by some that Michael had been up on the deck near the end, part of a crowd near the lifeboats, and that he had gone back down below for his pal Jim Reilly. I see him for the last time beside the lifeboats, and can believe the second bit only with a smile, a smile that greets the families of the sailors from Harris and Milton, who might believe this heroic act also to have been the final work of their own missing grandfathers.

A handful of medals came to Sydney Street in a cardboard postal box heavily stamped. My granny laid them in a drawer, and spoke little of Michael again. Or maybe she did do, and saved up her not-speaking for her grandchildren. When very young, sitting in a different house, in the street where the fish shop was, I'd ask her things, and she'd squint awkwardly, pressing her lips hard together till they formed a smile. Then she'd move on to other names and other times. I grew up with the sense that there was no family history, that only my brothers and I had stories of our own, and that there was something in the past of all my father's family that was dark and distressing. I wondered then what life had been for Michael and his many brothers and sisters – but my granny, a Catholic matriarch of the old stamp, was not the sort to open up to anyone on any subject not to do with Mass or soup.

It was clear without much saying it that the O'Hagans were not of her sort. She was jumpy and keen in front of us. It was plain. We were the O'Hagans. And she was, well, she was something apart from that. She had grown up amongst good-natured women; her father Hector Lavery had played for Clyde

FC, and he married again when Molly's mother died soon after giving birth to her. Her granny, Mary Mackenzie, had brought her up, and was apparently the great influence on her life. Molly, as far as I could see, was an O'Hagan only by marriage, and was never, even after many years, inclined to be one in character. She gave every impression of being a discreet, coping, religious, stern but fair old lady who'd seen too much and said too little.

I only saw her really express what you would call emotion once, and that was near the end of her life, when the illness that would kill her first set in. She sat with my mother one day and wept into a scrunched-up handkerchief. I came back and forth from inspecting a very lifelike statue of Mary, our Lady, in the bedroom next door. My granny was speaking like I'd never heard her do, in a way I found almost frightening. She seemed to trust my mother as far as she was able to, in the way that women who've lived in a similar relation to men sometimes do. They each held out a hand in front of the fire. 'I'm done,' my granny said. 'That's me finished.'

Molly's real name was Mary, and all her rent things and bits of paper had Mary O'Hagan typed on them. She went to Mass at St Mary's in the morning, coming back down Millroad Street with a carton of milk and something for the soup. She spent many a day looking after my cousin Desmond, who had a physical handicap, and who seemed to mean more to her than anyone below the clouds. One day, when my da had left me at my granny's house with a new dog that peed the carpet, my granny and me sat at the fire – without Desmond, who'd gone off to St Mungo's, the school up the road – and she showed me how to do the rosary. She wore slippers shaped like boots, with zips up the front. I asked her about St Mary's, her chapel, which stood on Abercrombie Street just over there. She lifted her rosary out of the cup of one hand, pinching the crucifix with the fingers of the other, letting the greenness and glassiness of the beads, unfurling in decades, birl and sway in front of me. Then she dropped them back into her palm, and smiled without teeth.

'Always go the chapel, son,' I think she said. 'Sundays, Holy Communion.'

She took out some pamphlets from a red missal, small rectangular glossies with pictures of Fathers and Sisters printed on. She was interested, I remember, in the Order of the Poor Clares and an order of monks whose name I forget, who were active in the parish of St Mary's. Molly was all for the Catholics; she wasn't a hater, really, but she thought the Protestants were surely bound for the darkness and she wouldn't have gone into a Protestant church for any amount of money. She would boycott a family wedding if not suitably apostolic, and she mourned, very quietly, the failure of all to live in the faith of her Church. Couples stuck together, so far as she was concerned. From her deathbed, she watched my brothers and me come and go from her, always in the company of a parent, but never with both together. Her cancer was far on, but her eyes shone out like beads.

As I grew up, I found it hard to imagine Molly as a wife or as a mother. I could only really see her the one way: as a granny and a sort of nun. I would eventually find it quite difficult to separate her ancient Glaswegian toughness, and her stony silence on the subject of the missing-presumed-dead Michael, from what I'd learned of the life of her namesake Sister Mary O'Hagan. Sister Mary would certainly have appealed to my granny, had she known her. She was a Poor Clare, who had founded the convent at Kenmure in the middle of the last century. The lettering on the cover of her biography, *In Memoriam*, is not unlike the gold text on Molly's missal. It has the baroque, tulip-entangled, pontifical look of the Catholic altar. The biographers praise the dedication and courage of their Holy Mother: 'The life of a Nun is a life of two loves,' they write, 'and it is too near the life of Christ, and has in it far too much of the humiliation of Bethlehem, and the pain of Calvary, to attract or please the world.'

My granny wasn't much interested in pleasing the world either, or letting the world please her. She would cheerily have hummed to these singers' Holy tunes. She was all for them. And closing all her windows down as tight as they'd go on the Twelfth of July – the steaming festival of the Orange Walk in Scotland – Molly would have gasped in empathy with those Sisters who noted how 'the Poor Clares were cruelly persecuted by the Calvinists under William of Orange'. Oh, yes, she'd say, uh-huh. 'It is related in our annals that one sister fell dead "because her pure ears could not bear the curses and blasphemies of his soldiers".'

My granny O'Hagan yearned for a better world than this one. But it was a world more like the one she'd known than she could have realized herself. Her paradise was not for everyone. Like earthly weddings and other good times, it could only be borne – and perhaps even borne lightly – if it was Catholic first to last. My granny had a good heart, but never a soft one. Like Sister Mary, she died surrounded by those who'd tried to love her, and whom she'd sometimes loved back. The Founding Sister of Kenmure is said to have gone very dark-lipped in her final moments, clutching at her cross, and praying hard. Eventually, she looked over at those gathered around. 'I know,' she said, 'the children I have reared.' The other Mrs Mary O'Hagan, my worn-out granny, didn't say much at the end, so far as I know. But her rosary beads were there, and most of her children were too.

THE GLASGOW MY grandparents grew up in no longer exists: it has disappeared. I suppose my sense of the family's missing history has always mingled with a sense that their world is missing in other ways too. Though I've never known much, I knew from quite early on – from hints, I suppose, and snatches of talk between aunts, from the way they'd roll their eyes, and from odd dreams I'd had – that if they ever stepped out of the dark, the lives of my Glasgow ancestors would tell me all I wanted to know about the city I'd been born into, and the people to whom I was born. People didn't move around much in Glasgow, or, at least, they didn't in the generations previous to my own, which has decanted and redeveloped in the usual modern ways. So to properly know your own family in an old city is to know something of the history of the city itself.

My paternal grandfather's people, gallivanting through the Calton of the twenties, were as hard as pig-iron. There were loads of them, in the usual Catholic way, and they ran their lives (and other people's) as if time were running out. Michael was drawn towards boxing, and he hung around the gym on Sydney Street, getting going as a manager. He was never taller than five feet four and a half, and was stocky, with a wide head, and arms a little stiff. In those days, men often boxed for quick money, and maybe also for quick fame, or romance, or instant power. The area clattered with the movements of the neatly named Fifty-Bob punchers; and title-fights were the heady stuff of day-dreams and nightmares. The diminutive king of this world was Benny Lynch, who grew up just across the Clyde, in the Gorbals. He was a champion, a real flashbulb, a role-model with a slicked-back middle-shed, and he died of drink before he got out of his thirties.

Michael got into boxing management with a pal called Thomas Gilmour. Gilmour's grandson, in my own time, would become the most visible manager-promoter in the city: full of top ideas, keen for the talent, and never shy of the camera. Our grandfathers signed a British Boxing Board of Control agreement which allowed them to represent a certain Francis McTigue of Lawmoor Street. The managers, the contract tells us, are expected to 'exercise every possible effort to secure contests and/or other avenues whereby the Boxer may profit, such as exhibition bouts, music hall, theatrical film contracts, or engagements as sparring assistant to other Boxers in training, or literary contributions to daily, weekly, monthly, annual or other publications, whether written actually by the said Boxer indicated, or merely such as for which he will accept the full responsibility . . .' And so on. I can only assume that the Conopticon Variety Theatre, minutes away in the Trongate, never resounded to the butting dance of Francis McTigue; nor, it appears, did he make it onto the pages of the *Daily Sketch*. The obscure and minimalist documentary world of East End professional boxing gives little word of him again, though there may have been flashes of glory unstilled by recordists and scribes.

People forever keen to have a pop at turning cash into cash saw boxing the same way they saw pitch-and-toss – it was a gambling game, though one more obviously sweaty and lethal. The boxers themselves, if good enough, and with luck on their side, could make money out of their talent; and good managers made it out of talent-spotting and opportunism. My granda, who was perhaps not the best at it, was on 10 per cent of everything between five and ten pounds, and 25 per cent of all earnings over a tenner. It was the punters' good judgement, of course, that made them money, but the size of their stakes would never have made them rich. Gambling was crooked but irresistible; and my granda was one of those done for practising it illegally. In later years, several of his brothers would seek to beat the licensed betting shops, by methods cannier than the services of good judgement could provide, and some of them were imprisoned in Barlinnie for it.

Michael's mother was born in Glasgow, but her people came from Belfast. His father, Hugh O'Hagan, trained as an iron-worker and lived on the road where St Mary's Chapel stood, Abercrombie Street, number 112. Hugh died of bronchitis at his work in 1932: he'd been working as a night watchman with the Statute Labour Department in Govan. All his sons went to Borstal, and graduated to Barlinnie Prison, though none for ever. A few months in Michael's case; a few years in his young brother James's. At one time, though, in the early thirties, it is said there were four of the brothers in prison at the same time. They were convicted for theft or safe-blowing or agitation of one sort or another. Hugh's father was called Hugh as well, and had been born in Glasgow in 1842, at a time when the Irish were flocking to the west coast of Scotland in their tens of thousands, running from famine and hopelessness. Hugh Sr's parents – Hugh O'Hagan and Helen McQuade – may have seen the trouble coming, for they departed County Tyrone a few years before the Famine began, and set up a hide- and skin-dealing concern in the High Street. All of the women worked, mostly as seamstresses, slipper-makers, steam-loom weavers, or rollers of tobacco; few of them could write, signing their Catholic marriage certificates with an X.

A weird skew, typical of nineteenth-century cities, saw thousands of straitened in-comers settling in the east of the city. Clydeside industrialists – Charles Randolph, David Tod, John Elder – gave them work in their mammoth shipyards, over to the west; others went to engineering, to factories hissing with industry, to forges and all the rest now quiet or gone. When the *Queen Mary* passed up the Clyde in 1936, she was moving through thirty-five feet of water, a depth created by engineers, who'd been dredging the bottom for years. In my own time, because of what's happened, because of the death of the big industries, we've been given to singing a kind of hymn to Glasgow's industrial might. And yes, you'd need a heart like a swinging brick to sneer at the magnificence of those ships and those engines, or to deny the human effort they embodied. But the price was high; and the life, for many, was pretty desperate. Now that the shipyards are gone, we might rightly reflect on the proud launch-days and glories of a construction era too sorely missed. Yet from time to time, I wonder if that eulogy includes enough recognition of the many working lives used up – not quite seen, not quite missed – under the wondrous bows of those ships. We might well be helpless before the romance of the Clyde shipyards, and we may be fairly entitled to that – but it is our romance, not that of those who worked there. Our worklessness can make all work look heaven-sent.

My mother's father would have known what I mean. He spent the best part of a decade without work, waiting in line at the docks, and outside other gates, for casual work that was tough, and tough to find, in the years after 1920, before the next war. Charlie Docherty, nicknamed Beef, came from a family of

Patricks and Gilroys – on his father's side – and a bunch of Wilsons, Frasers, and Grays on the other. Agnes Wilson, his mother, was a hair-factory worker (cleaning and treating horsehair for mattress-stuffing) and a Protestant, and he took from her his elegant nose and wide, clear eyes. But all was not to keep well with the eyes. A fight broke out at his Calton corner one night, as Beef was up the stairs with a book. A crowd had formed, and some of them shouted for him to come down, quickly come down, and break up the fight, which had grown thick and vicious, the way street-fights can do, surrounded by eggers-on. He got involved, trying to pull the terriers apart, when some panting well-wisher threw in a ginger bottle, which bashed off the wall and lodged a slither of itself in Beef's right eye. When the glass came out, at the Royal Infirmary, the eye had to come out too. In time, it was replaced by a glass one, a polished globe, which shines out from old pictures, giving him the dandified, quizzical look of some cinema grandfather. At night (my granny Doc told me) he'd place the thing in a blue tumbler.

I never saw my granda Docherty either, though he lived on in holiday pictures and in my granny Doc's conversation in ways that made me feel fairly acquainted. His countenance, even if just in my own head, was as sunny as Michael's was dark. Beef was a singer of Irish songs, a borrower of books, and a merchant seaman who made it home to Glasgow, where he got some work as an engineer's labourer and later as a clerk. As well as this, he liked to sip beer, and he did that, without grief or care, at the Steps Bar in Glassford Street, until his heart failed him half way through the sixties. As he walked home from work that night, he cut down past St Mary's – the chapel where his parents were married, Agnes having 'turned' – and made his way down Stevenston Street, where he met his son-in-law, who saw that his breath was short and his tie all loose, and took him into the house. My mother never forgot the shortness of his breath that evening; years later, whenever we bumped into someone who rasped like that, my mum's hand would go up to her throat, as if on its own, and she'd look at us, saying: 'That's what my daddy was like at the end of his days.'

Charlie was probably shadowed a little by Beef, his gamely young self: he was no stranger to the world he lived in. But family life seemed to have him in its grip; it reformed him; it placed him in a new relation to his surroundings – he was a father, and a husband who loved his wife – and the old temptations must have lost their shine. Michael, it seems, never really got to that point.

There's no telling just how much and just what kind of competition grew up between Michael and his brothers. None of them escaped themselves, or each other, until one, Willy Andrew, absconded to Manchester and made a separate life there. The family 'madness' people spoke of – 'the mad O'Hagans' – was, whatever it was, the name given to the kind of behaviour displayed by Michael's brothers and doubtless by Michael as well. They were all into it. They moved in fluid motion, all of them, between sport-as-gambling and gambling-as-extortion; between drinking for courage and drinking through remorse; between thieving for glory and stealing for need; between politicking through strength of religion and faith and agitating through love of anarchy and strife. As the thirties progressed, there would be spells for each of the O'Hagan boys – and some of the girls – when they would find themselves in the throes of a full-blown dependence. James had seven previous convictions on 19 March 1935, when he was arrested, aged twenty-nine, and given twenty-one months with hard labour for trying to rob premises at 335 St Vincent Street. He was armed with knives and explosives. A year and a half to the day, out of prison early, he was arrested again. The following article appeared in the *Glasgow Herald* under the headline 'Reputed Thief Caught in Glasgow':

> The maximum sentence for the offence – three months' imprisonment with hard labour – was imposed at Glasgow central police court yesterday on James O'Hagan, who admitted a charge that, being a suspected person and reputed thief, he was found loitering in an enclosed yard at 22–24 Armour Street with intent to commit theft and house-breaking.
>
> It was stated that on Saturday night the police got a telephone message that premises at 22 Armour Street were being broken into. When the police got there they saw the accused climbing an outside stairway leading to a doorway in a sausage factory. When charged he said: 'I was looking for some ready cash.'

The main thoroughfare in the Calton is called the Gallowgate. It runs all the way from Glasgow Cross to Parkhead, where Celtic Football Club have their hallowed ground. Not long before James O'Hagan was sent down for the attempted robbery at the nearby Armour Street, my granda Michael (then working as a pool-table coverer) was involved in an event that would put him in Barlinnie for six months. There were hardmen around the Gallowgate in the twenties and thirties – there still are today – who were distinguishable by their shortness, their awful neatness, and their ability to smoke with one side of their mouth whilst speaking through the other. Michael was one of these little Cagneys; he was all for his own people, they tell me, and he only did harm to himself. The thing that sent him to Barlinnie (he'd been before, but never for so long) was his spell marauding the streets in the company of a gun, which he fired, and which is said not to have belonged to him. Michael was doing some work for publicans in the Gallowgate; and whatever it was it was the sort of work made easier with the help of a revolver. Michael's world was full of promise and disappointment; the gun may have eased him, or it may have eased his way in some shadowy deal or other.

I can't tell. But as his world began to open up to me, I thought I began to see why it had always been shrouded in dusk. Simply: it was that sort of world; not the sort that people discussed openly with the wider circle of the family, and not the sort expected to make the children beam with pride. Not so simply: it was a world that had never entirely receded. If the accounts of it were missing – missing to the extent that even the participants didn't know the background – it was for a reason. If it had been as dead as history, and finished, then we would have known all about it, we'd have laughed and turned over the bizarre novelty of our origins. But that couldn't happen. We had no history, I now think, because that stuff was never seen as gone. To talk of it, to bring it back, was to speak too loudly – and too directly – of present troubles. Better to remain a little in the dark, they seemed to say, as to live too much in the glaring light of the truth, and all that it might suggest. Some families are just like that.

*

IN MAY 1921, something happened in the Calton, something involving the Chapel of St Mary's, and guns, and Sinn Fein, my grandfather, and his Uncle Francis, a confectioner. The story, in its way, tells us much of what the O'Hagan brothers had to live up to, in a time and a place where living up to the family name was everything. The story could not really be told before, not properly, as many of the papers were out of sight, and the matter was silenced a long time ago. The history of Sinn Fein in Glasgow – that sometimes boiling community of socialist-Catholics and Ulster Orangemen – has, for the most part, been erased from the city's account of itself. In the twenties, it was much more than a matter of one or two households and the zealous machinations of the families within. It was a faith – a bitter creed for some – scribbled into the very pavements around St Mary's.

Michael was living with his parents at 112 Abercrombie Street – St Mary's stood at 89 – in that spring of 1921. He was eighteen, and spending a lot of his time with James Burns, who lived at number 77, and who would stand as Michael's witness five years later, when he married my grandmother Mary Lavery, a quiet girl with beautiful hair, then living in Stirling Street. An Irish pal of theirs, Vincent Campbell, lived alone with his da, one stair up, in the tenement at number 74. It was right across the street from the house of Jamie Burns and his family. Hanging at the corner, Michael and Jamie would sometimes see the Campbells nip in and out of the different closes, looking people up. Michael's uncle Francis was a pal of the older Campbell. At fifty-six, though, Francis O'Hagan was older than any of them.

Ten minutes past noon on Wednesday 4 May 1921, a black wagon pulled out of the police headquarters at St Andrew's Square. Inside, there were two prisoners, who were held in separate cabins. One of them called himself Frank Somers, though his real name was Frank J. Carty. He'd appeared in front of Stipendiary Neilson at the Central Police Court that morning, and was remanded in custody until the following Saturday. Carty had broken out of Sligo Jail in June 1920, had stolen a revolver, and had later broken out of the jail at Derry. He was wanted in Belfast.

The van, perhaps for reasons that will become obvious – but which were, at the time, unmentioned in all written communications – had a fairly heavy escort that day. It made its way into the Saltmarket, rumbled past Glasgow Cross, and headed onto the High Street leading to Duke Street Prison. Constable Thomas Rose was driving the van in uniform. George Stirton sat next to him; he'd made note of the time on the Tolbooth clock as they passed: it was twelve minutes after noon. McDonald, the Detective Inspector, peered right ahead next to him – both he and Stirton were in plain clothes. Robert Johnston sat tight at the end of the cab, with his leg over the side, resting on the mucky footboard. As they passed over George Street, and began to move up the scuffed and cobbled incline they call the Bell o' the Brae, Johnston's eye fell on a run of thick white lettering above the street corner on his side: *Globe Loan Office*, it said. Rose, the driver, was whistling then, and on his side, on the opposite corner from where Johnston looked, stood a building shorter than the tenements around it: *The Paraffin Oil and Colour Store* was emblazoned across the front, between the windows. As the van ran over the top half of the Brae, the Scotstoun tram passed them on the other side. Rose reached down to change gear, about to turn right into the Drygate, at the junction of High Street, Castle Street, and Rottenrow, where the prison gates stood.

The van was cornered. With revolvers cracking, packs of men ran out from the south-west corner of Cathedral Square; others emerged from Rottenrow; more from alleys and closes situated near the top of the High Street. Bullets sank into the front of the van, some flew past, bouncing off the prison wall. A gunman called Mooney took aim, and fired at the side of the cabin. Inspector Johnston dropped out of the van, and lay dead on the ground. The van skidded to a halt, and Stirton jumped off, letting fire at the assailants from his own revolver. Within seconds, he was hit on the wrist of his right hand, and he dropped the gun. Three shots banged into the van's radiator, as MacDonald blazed his way round the side, stooping low, staking out a position in the gun-fight. The attacking fire was coming from the front and the sides. The windscreen crashed inward at the same time as some of the ambushers fired into the keyholes of the locks on the van's rear doors. But the thing held. Frank Carty lay flat inside the van; the second prisoner panicked, banging around inside, and shouting for help. Within three minutes, the attackers, seeing that the doors were jammed, scattered. They made their escapes in all directions, through alleys, up close-mouths, off round the back of the Corporation Water Pumping Station (which stood on the opposite side of the road), and some dipped down the banking of the old Molendinar Burn, disappearing behind Glasgow Cathedral and up over the antique burial site known as the Necropolis. It was a matter of seconds, that's all it was, and they'd all disappeared.

Then as now, unemployed men would gather in Cathedral Square to drink and pass the time. Some of them heard the banging, but thought it came from some back-firing motor. Schoolchildren coming along during their midday break were frightened by the noise; some ran into shops and houses. A few people said they witnessed the attack itself. They saw Sergeant Stirton chasing a rabble of escaping men up Rottenrow, and saw others as they made their way across Cathedral Square. There was one young man, a witness observed, a stout, dark-haired fellow stuffing a revolver into his pocket as he strode away. He was as pale as a sheet. Very white, this young man, as he made his escape. He got away through Cats' Close, a thin, uneven passageway which cut through the tenements behind the High Street. As the scene cleared, and the van hobbled through Duke Street Prison's gates, all eyes turned to the forty-one-year-old body of Inspector Johnston, which lay bleeding and motionless between two tram-lines.

Late in the afternoon police came to St Mary's, looking for the Revd. Father Patrick McRory. He was a young, very handsome priest, well known and liked among the parish; he was often to be seen in and out of the houses in the Calton, especially those in Abercrombie Street. The officers went to number 74 and arrested Patrick Campbell and his son Vincent – there were a number of men in the house who they arrested at the same time; they sent another company of officers up the road, to arrest Francis O'Hagan. At number 74, they'd found a revolver and six rounds of ammunition. Arrests were made elsewhere in the street, and in other streets bordering the Gallowgate. One of those arrested along with the Campbells during the raid at 74 Abercrombie Street was James Mitchell, a twenty-nine-year-old known Republican who had been seen early in the afternoon of the shooting, using the telephone at the Ivanhoe Hotel in Buchanan Street (Douglas 3486). The taxi company of Messrs Wylie & Lochead received a telephone call from Thomas Tracey, an undertaker and carriage hirer in Bridgeton (later a prisoner), requesting that a taxi cab be sent to pick up James Mitchell – and unnamed others – at the Ivanhoe Hotel and to deliver him to Abercrombie Street. A certain Mr McKechnie was sent to do the job. On returning to the Wylie & Lochead office he told his boss, Mr Cochrane, that he felt sure the people he was driving had something to do with the 'Sinn Fein outrage' in the High Street, news of which had, by this time, spread all over the city.

This information led to the arrest of the Campbells, Mitchell, Tracey, some associates and partners, and my Great-Great-Uncle Francis. McKechnie, the driver, was very nervous of passing the information on to the police. He was reluctant to become involved any further, and had almost to be dragged in to view an identification parade later that day, at the head-quarters in St Andrew's Square. Later that evening, his boss wrote a letter to the Chief Constable which spoke of a near-breakdown in McKechnie. 'The experience,' said the letter, 'has occasioned a mental depression, which has led to a fear of his life.' Many other witnesses had expressed a similar fear, a pure horror at the thought of retaliation, and this was to prove very significant when it came to the trial. 'It is regrettable,' wrote the Chief Constable to the Secretary of State for Scotland, 'to see the witnesses yielding to the threats of Sinn Fein.'

Sarah Kerr, of 92 Abercrombie Street, was among those who spread the word that police had gone into St Mary's Chapel armed with handguns and rifles. One outrage, they whispered then shouted, was being met with another. Dozens of Catholic families went spare, and poured onto the street, as news of Father McRory's arrest spread. At this time, around 9 p.m., twenty people had been arrested in the area, suspected of having been involved in the gun-battle and the murder of Inspector Johnston. Michael O'Hagan went from house to house, looking for news, wondering if an alibi could be established for Francis in the event that he might need one. A large crowd, over two thousand strong by then, had gathered outside the chapel-house, and were incandescent with fury, throwing stones and bottles, and cursing the police. The crowd was riotous, assaulting any police officer who came too near, and some had begun to run up the Gallowgate in mobs, smashing the windows of pubs and restaurants and banks. Leon Jaffe, who owned a cobbler's at 588 Gallowgate, later complained to police that three pairs of boots had been stolen from his shop window. As the riot flared, the Chief Constable asked for assistance from the military; he was sent a sergeant and ten soldiers, who were to stay in the area until the 'Sinn Fein prisoners', as they were called, had been installed in Duke Street prison. Late in the evening, as a tramcar made its way down Abercrombie Street, it was ambushed by a crowd of young men, who smashed the windows, and kicked in the metal, bawling and spitting at the alarmed passengers cowering inside.

Robert Johnston's murder, in the broad daylight of Rotten-row, brought a great deal of feeling against Irish Catholics and their Glaswegian offspring, some of which has never entirely gone. The riot in the East End seemed, to many, like the behaviour of a community quick to vindicate murder, a community neither Scottish nor British, but one rotten-in-exile, clannish, and pious only about the alleged desecration of their own church. Violence, at first glance, seemed to be an acceptable part of their world, if not of their nature. The East End, for ever after, would carry a reputation for easy killing and a tolerance of needless suffering. The Catholics bore this hardest, bore it as a legend and as a reality, each feeding the other, as if the body and blood of Christ were only the opening lesson.

27

The idea has lasted into my own time, this idea of Holy Revenge, of blood being shared beneath the Catholic altar, and spilled on the streets beyond, all in the altar's name. Father McRory left prison before long, and returned to the anxious parishioners around Abercrombie Street. He never opened his mouth and he died in 1929, of a burst appendix. My granny O'Hagan took me one day – fifty years on – down the stone steps of St Mary's, both of us fresh from a Communion I barely understood. She held my hand, and her eyes blinked in the sun. I knew she had glass rosary beads in her pocket, and a bone for the soup in her bag.

My relative escaped conviction for the Sinn Fein atrocity: the curious Scottish verdict of 'not proven' was delivered in all thirteen cases committed for trial. Francis O'Hagan was thought to be of unsound mind, and he returned to the Calton to live out his distempered days. Worries about Sinn Fein activity on Scotland's west coast, however, were brought to a head by all this, and opponents were keen to see the Fenian problem stamped out without delay. For several years following the trial, a great many politicians, military people, and Protestant churchmen ached with a sense of injustice, and they fulminated broadly against the 'threat' of zealous Catholicism. The spirit of this was embodied in the harassment, and eventual internment, of East End Catholics in 1924. The murder of Inspector Johnston was met, over time, by alternative brutalities wrought against people who weren't involved, but who were people who might have shared something with those who were. There was a strong feeling against them, against all of them. The report to the General Assembly of the Church of Scotland, presented at Edinburgh in 1923, less than a year before the internments began, had this to say on the subject of the Catholic threat:

In no other European country did the Reformation have a more complete triumph than in Scotland. It was not until large numbers of Irish Roman Catholics came over from Ireland that the Roman Catholic Church began to grow, to feel her power, and to assert her influence, and this was the beginning of the destruction of the unity and homogeneity of the Scottish people ... The Irish race too modify admirable Scottish customs. The Scottish reverence for the Sabbath day is passing away; it has now become a day for political meetings and for concerts [. . .] The Roman Catholic Church [. . .] has her missioners in Glasgow, able men, who exhibit the doctrines of Rome in guises calculated to persuade and convince Protestant minds.

With the establishment of the Free State in Ireland, magistrates and Church of Scotland leaders had been both fearful and hopeful: fearful of new terrorist activity on the land they liked to call the mainland; and hopeful that many Irish Catholics would go back home now that home was approximately free. As it turned out, few went back; many of the 'Irish Catholics' in Glasgow had never seen Ireland, though they often cared a great deal for the political trouble there. That caring would appear to have been on the rise in the months leading up to the ambush of the police wagon, and the riot which followed the arrests. The authorities, for their part, saw something coming in 1920, and the heavy hand they brought down after 1921 might be seen not only as a reaction to the Glasgow outrage, but as a belated recognition that they had responded softly to their own early warnings.

'I desire to bring before the Cabinet,' wrote Lord Novar, the Scottish Secretary, in a government memorandum dated 18

October 1920, 'an aspect of Sinn Fein activity in the west of Scotland which calls for attention.' He had for some time been receiving reports, from all over the west coast, which detailed attempts by 'well-dressed men' to smuggle explosives to Ireland; many firms, in Glasgow and Clydebank and Alloa, had contacted the police with their suspicions, and with fears as to the security of their plants. Captain H. J. Despard, of the Lanarkshire Constabulary, wrote a letter on 9 December. 'Men sympathetic to the cause,' he reported, 'are known to have as their main function the collection of money to send over to Ireland ... I consider that firm combined action of the Police Authorities concerned, by which the arrest of the leading Sinn Feiners in Scotland is secured, would put a stop to the whole movement in Scotland.'

Anxiety was on the up, and those with an interest were keeping a look out. Glasgow's Procurator Fiscal made notes on anything he heard about the dreaded Sinn Feiners – he would send out companies of detectives to gather information – and he wrote them up into reports, hectic manuscripts which have been missing from Glasgow's story of itself, rubbed from the city's stock of social truths, for seventy-five years. They are tight and elegant documents, often remaining only in the smudged lilac print of carbon, with curly letterheads and weird telegraph names over the top. They are the sorts of documents whose headings say slightly more than the contents; like the cumbersome titles on pamphlets by English Levellers of the seventeenth century, they are comically long, unwieldy, and precise: *A Letter from John Lamb, Scottish Office, Whitehall, W.1, About the Fear of Sinn Fein Blowing Up the Admiralty Fuel Installation Extending from the Clyde to the Firth of Forth. The Need for a Battalion, Davenport 'B', to Protect the Explosives at Ardeer and Irvine*. But the reports of the Procurator Fiscal must have made alarming reading in the closing months of 1920:

> It appears that on the 11 September, a body of about 100 men arrived by train at Lennoxtown, and having proceeded to Campsie, which is in the vicinity, they camped there for the night. It is probable that most of those men were from Glasgow [...] My information is that the men were drilled (some shots were fired) and later attended Mass and that the Clergyman who officiated reprimanded them for coming there. It has been ascertained that on the same evening (Sunday, 12 September) they hired a char-a-bancs in which they were conveyed from Campsie to the car terminus at Bishopbriggs where they dispersed. They no doubt completed the journey into the city by tramcar.

The Procurator's informants lost the corps at that point, among the various public conveyances of September 1920, and could follow them no further. The crowd of young men, I imagine, fresh from drilling and Holy Communion, may have made their way at that point to St Andrew's Halls, where the biggest Sinn Fein demonstration ever to occur in Glasgow took place that night. The main hall, built to hold five thousand people, was full; Berkeley Hall, which adjoined it, held another thousand. About two thousand people were unable to find a place inside. They stayed out on the street, and were addressed by various speakers visible only by gaslight. The chairman of the principal meeting was Joseph Brown, and the speakers, over from Ireland, were Sean McFergus and Sean Mulroy. There was no small delegation at this event, both on the pews and out on the streets, from that area to the east encircling the Gallowgate.

It was a serious business, this. In my own twenties – far enough from the twenties I've been telling you about – a sort of peace would break out in Ireland, and Sinn Fein would be sort of accepted as diplomats and politicians. I say 'sort of' both times, and that's what I mean. The suspicion of old methods – resentment at past evils – may be filtered away over decades. In Glasgow, I'm sure it takes longer. Resentment between Catholics and Protestants in Scotland thrives much as before: Sinn Fein are still murderers, and Orangemen and Unionists are still blue-nosed heathens. But the sense of imminent threat is long gone; no bombs go off in Glasgow these days, and none are expected; there is no political struggle, it's just all personal. But in 1920 there was a sense that terrorism could be happening; it was taking up a position in the life of the city. To most of those passing secret memos, it looked like a hatred was taking hold – resentment of a kind likely to make the twin venoms of the tribes of Celtic and the warriors of Rangers look like sport. On the evening of Saturday 11 September, the day before the show of strength at St Andrew's Halls, a certain quantity of gelignite was placed close to the north gable wall of the police station in Chester Street, Shettleston. It was ignited, causing a large hole in the ground, and shaking the foundations of the building. Inspector Robert Johnston, murdered the following year at Rottenrow, may have heard the blast – he lived only a couple of streets away.

A week after this, an informal meeting of Glasgow's Ulster Volunteers and Orangemen argued and worried over the threat. They'd heard about the drilling and firing at Campsie Glen, and were just learning of St Andrew's Halls. They decided to offer a large body of men to assist the Glasgow police in putting a stop to it. Informers and amateur detectives began to spring up, passing information on to an increasingly vigilant police force. The Director of Intelligence at Scotland House in London was inundated with scraps of talk, overheard plans, obscure documents, transcripts of hostile speeches, and that sort of thing. Everything was marked 'Confidential' and kept under wraps. A meeting was held late in the evening in Greenock, he'd heard, where thirty-seven Sinn Fein clubs were represented, and where twenty-two commandants were present. The informer went on: 'It was stated that there are over 30,000 Sinn Fein volunteers in Glasgow and the West of Scotland; that 20,000 had revolvers and 2,000 had rifles, and that there was an abundance of ammunition.' He paused to catch his breath. 'It was also stated that they had plans of Maryhill Barracks and Hamilton Barracks and all the Drill Halls in Glasgow.' The Sheriff of Renfrewshire received a letter from H. C. Ferguson, Secretary of the Clyde Valley Electrical Power Company. It expressed their fear of imminent attack by Sinn Fein, and requested military or police protection. 'This station,' he went on, 'forms part of a system, from which electricity is supplied to a large number of the steelworks, engineering works and collieries in Lanarkshire, and to the shipyards and engineering works on the Clyde.' At the bottom of the letter, scribbled in black, are the words of the Chief Constable: 'A large number of employees at these works are either Irish or of Irish extraction.'

MY GREAT-GRANNY Dunn was born Euphemia Campbell in 1893. She worked as a hawker in the Calton, selling second-hand cloth in Paddy's Lane just off the Saltmarket. When she was married, in 1911, she was living at 248 Gallowgate, and when asked by the priest in the chapel of St Alphonsus what he'd to put down as her occupation, she swithered, and said 'rag-store worker'. As she stood at the altar with Thomas Dunn, Famie was eight months pregnant; her eldest daughter, my mother's mum, Agnes Kelly Dunn, was born within five weeks. The Thomas Dunn who walked up the aisle of St Alphonsus with his pregnant wife would, twenty years later, eject his second daughter Mary from the house, and expel her from the family, for falling pregnant to a local boyfriend. Mary went to America, to a new life, but gave it all up to come back to the Gallowgate and deal with family troubles. You still see her from time to time, a very old lady now, still unmarried, trailing her past behind her like a dead weight.

The Gallowgate that my great-granny Dunn brought children into was a place increasingly given over to matters of buying and selling. People sold fruit and fish off the back of carts and barras; lace and buttons and second-hand frocks came out of a number of tied bundles laid out on the pavement. The City Improvement Schemes had been patchy in their effectiveness; most of the tenements were still crooked and black, the rows crumbling into powder. Some Calton cottages (built when the area was called Blackfaulds) still stood, like concaving pavilions to the slums behind. Some of my mother's forebears lived at 44 Havannah Street in the Candleriggs, a horrible place outdoing the backcourts of the High Street, and the worst of the bevelled tenements at Edinburgh's Haymarket, for hopelessness and stink. A certain Dr Brown, writing in his official returns for 1844: 'Sixty-four Havannah Street is not surpassed by any close in the city for filth, misery, crime and disease; it contains 59 houses, all inhabited by a most wretched class of individuals ... 105 Havannah Street was an old carpet factory, lately arranged into 36 cells about 7 feet square ... comfort, convenience, and ventilation kept out of sight.'

His colleague of the time, Dr David Smith, wrote of the area at the base of the Gallowgate. 'Need I add,' he adds, 'that the inhabitants with whom I have to deal are of the very lowest ranks in society; a few of them are labourers, but the greatest majority are hawkers and beggars, thieves and prostitutes.' Reading over the notes of Dr Smith, you get the distinct impression of someone not entirely happy at their work. His pen takes another turn across the page. 'Fever,' he scribbles, 'fever abounds.'

Things weren't that bad in Famie's day. There was a bit more work, more medicine, and just a little more of society. By 1928, the partly covered market in the Gallowgate, the 'Barras', which had started as a titchy market-place in Greendyke Street, was fully covered over, and sides were added a few years later. The great entrepreneur of the Barras was Margaret McIver, who made a mint out of its expansion. She turned it into the biggest free-trade market in Glasgow, and it became the focal point for the community around it. People knew people who worked there; the stuff that was sold off as new would some day come back second-hand. People's lives – not everyone's, but many's – circulated round the life of the market, and the life of the pubs that dotted away from it all the way up the Gallowgate. It was like that, only more so, after Christmas Eve 1934, when Maggie McIver built the Barrowland Ballroom on top of the covered market. It would become one of the most famous and famously well-attended dance halls in the country. It lived there at the centre of things: B-a-r-r-o-w-l-a-n-d. With a neon flash that burned its way into the future.

IN 1923, PRISON warders in Glasgow – at Duke Street Jail and at Barlinnie – were debating whether they should be permitted to carry revolvers or rifles. Worries over a Sinn Fein assault were at a pitch, and several commercial companies were enjoying the armed police protection they'd asked for. Francis O'Hagan was drinking and staying out of the way; Michael was boxing, seeing his girlfriend, and keeping quiet. The rumblings around town, that something was going to happen, came true in early March, when detachments of police officers raided the homes of several persons in and around the Calton – and some others in the Govan and Partick areas to the west and south. James Hickey, who ran a shop at 492 Gallowgate, was pulled out of his bed, cuffed, and driven away in a van. Patrick Murray, of 58 Crown Street, was woken the same way; his house was searched and he was taken and confined in an unknown place. They – along with seventy-eight others living in Scotland – were arrested under the Restoration of Order in Ireland Regulations, and it was decided that they should be deported forthwith, and interned in Mountjoy Military Prison in Dublin. The men were stowed on HMS *Wolfhound*, HMS *Viceroy*, and HMS *Castor*, and were taken immediately to Ireland.

A joint appeal was lodged the next day with the Secretary of State for Scotland. James Hickey wrote a letter to the Home Office. 'I am a British subject,' it starts out, 'born in Glasgow, 21 July 1879. I have lived all my life in Glasgow. I have never been a member of any organization, political or otherwise. This internment means financial ruin to me, as I have a wife and three children depending on me, and no-one to look after my small business, which has gone to the wall.' After a few weeks, the wives appealed to the Glasgow Parish Council, asking for subsistence money. The wife of Patrick Murray later wrote to George Buchanan, her MP. 'My family consist of seven children,' she said, 'the youngest 2 and a half years and eldest 18 years. I have only one girl working earning 14/- per week. My boy is getting 15/- per week unemployment money and I get 30/- per week from Parish, total income £2:19:0 per week. One of my children is a cripple having lost his leg six years ago. Up till the time my husband was deported he was employed with North British Railway Coy. at Bellgrove Station.'

Buchanan did what he could with the Secretary of State; James Maxton MP did the same, on behalf of Mrs Hickey and her children. They were worried about the manner in which the families were suffering. Lord Novar wrote back to Maxton soon after: 'As regards the position of Hickey's wife and children, there is no special provision for the maintenance of the dependents of persons interned and in case of destitution application would require to be made to the Parish Council for relief.'

Hickey was transferred to Brixton Prison, in London, and was called before the Irish Deportees Committee on 4 May. Hickey is called into the room by the chairman, Lord Trevethin.

Trevethin: Take a seat, Hickey . . . Well, you are a dealer in what, at Glasgow?

Hickey: I am an agent in barbed wire, fencing wire and general ironmongery. I have a licence to deal in firearms from the Glasgow Police. I became an agent for a firm called A.G. Baird, 74 York Street, Glasgow. Now the grounds I appeal on are these. I never was a member at any time of any political organization whatever.

Trevethin: That is very wise.

Hickey: I can produce witnesses, Detective Inspector Niven of the Glasgow Police, Detective Constable . . .

Trevethin: They could not tell what your sympathies were.

Hickey: I do not take part in any politics. I always uphold the government of the people of the country, a Constitutionalist.

Trevethin: That is a very wise point of view.

Hickey was released from Brixton on 18 May, and he headed back to the Gallowgate. Another of the internees, Art O'Brien, won an appeal against the Home Office, which created much embarrassment with the government, who later ruled that all the internees at Mountjoy should be sent home. They were brought across from Holyhead on 17 May aboard a ship called HMS *Mayfield*. It arrived at nine thirty in the morning and police quickly made arrangements with the Free State troops for the internees to come ashore in packs. The Glaswegian men came out first, accompanied on the three-hundred-yard walk to the booking office by a small guard of soldiers. The prisoners were each given a train ticket to the station nearest their home, and were told they were free to do as they pleased. Some, we hear, were abusive to the officers, spitting and shouting the odds, while others were silent as they stood on the platform, staring along the track to where it bent round the corner.

I WAS BORN in 1968, in Duke Street Hospital. It seems it was a fine year to be new in; everything was changing, and the Glasgow of before was being battered into another shape. Giant tower blocks, and new housing developments, were rising (as they liked to say) out of the rubble. They had been going up since the end of the war, really, but 1968 was a sort of year zero: the past was being stamped out, areas were being cleared and made new. Most of the change was planned, and much of it was hoped for. And the gods seemed all for it too: a great storm swept across the city the Friday I arrived, making thousands of shoogly tenements in an instant uninhabitable. I think of my mother staring at a wet window that Saturday morning in Duke Street Maternity, and promising that this fourth boy of hers would be the very, very last.

Fire and the end of history made the cover of the London *Times* that day. 'Student rioters,' it blared, 'set fire to the telephone cabins of the Paris Stock Exchange in a wave of violence which spread to a dozen different corners of the capital.' It's sometimes a long way from one's world to the world; and Glasgow – the place, the weather, the talk, the people – had always assumed itself to be somewhere out of the way. But the Glaswegian air I first inhaled in May 1968 – as locally thick as it was – had a distinct something in it, and much of what characterizes the city nowadays arose out of decisions made in that year.

Glasgow has, for this long while, not liked its myths. An age is upon us now that thinks of cities as having an image, a corporate face, that winks at investors, smiles at shoppers, and blushes in the company of those who know better. That's OK. But the city's account of itself will sometimes need awakening. It may require some truthful inelegance to break in unannounced, and interrupt the endlessly cleansing new-way-of-doing-things. It's not bad, not bad at all, that a city should want to better its past, that it should want to blossom and improve. But public relations, in civic life, should be kept in check by the public to whom it relates. The struggle over questions of renewal in Glasgow is mainly a battle over social history; there are those who would care for a truer picture than is currently fashionable, knowing that a free hand with the airbrush serves to mask not only historical madness and inequity, but obliterates present troubles too.

1968 was the high point of New. The little world around the Gallowgate swayed to a different tune, but the past would always come dancing by, reminding all who could notice, all who could see, that old gangs never die – they just buy new suits, or pass on their old ones to younger gods with smarter troubles and haircuts. The area's bits of bad past – to do with religion, fighting, money-lending, and gangsterism – had dropped mostly out of sight during the war years, and come tumbling back in the late fifties and sixties. To look at the buildings, the past seemed over, done, eradicated. The trams were gone, tenements were being cheerfully ground to dust, motorway planners were cutting the city centre into hexagonal clumps, and a wee lassie from Thomson Street called Lulu was still making everybody feel all right with a breathless number called 'Shout!'. The past was put out of sight, swallowed up by all our likely tomorrows. That's what they say, that's how they tell it, the legions of those-who-were-there. But, really, Glasgow's past was never far removed: people wore its detail in the very expressions, the words and faces, that they toured round the city's streets.

Gallowgate's market had grown still more by the sixties, and the dancehall above it was infamous. By the year I was born, though, the street was lined with shops never heard of in the twenties. The first fourteen odd-numbered units in the street were taken up by Woodhouse's Furniture Stores, attached to the Crystal Bells pub. As you walked up the street in that year, on the opposite side from the Barrowland, you'd pass the Plasterers' Hall, then up past the National Restaurant, where men would wait for work. Van and lorry drivers up from the south would park here, and sometimes they'd hire a local man like Harry Carrigan, who'd sit in their cab for a price, and lead the drivers to their various drop-off points around the city. Up the road further, and you'd pass the Caledonian Clothing Co., then Scotstoun Steam Laundry. Across the road from here was the pend where Famie Dunn had lived in the twenties and well after that. The close is boarded-up now: my great-granny Famie died seventeen days after I was born. By quite a distance, she was the last of her generation in my family, and the only remnant of the nineteenth century.

Up past the Barrowland, on the same side, at the corner of Elcho Street, was the Royal Bank of Scotland. In 1968, like many buildings in the area, it was being altered and extended and broken down. On the night of the East End riot – one of the forgotten nights of May 1921 – the building was called the British Linen Bank, and its windows were smashed to smithereens by the mob. The then manager, whose name has gone, wrote to the Magistrates Committee of the old Corporation of Glasgow, asking that the Linen Bank be reimbursed for damage to plate-glass done by the invisible rioters. The building renewing itself in the late sixties, spreading back into the car park, had windows up high and covered in wire. Right across the road was the Meatmarket, whose giant gates were crowned with wrought-iron patterning set in a half-moon. A bull's head, in plaster, looked down from the very top. My da had worked here as an animal killer before I was born.

In those days it was possible – if you didn't fancy a high rise – to get into one of the newly renovated houses off Duke Street, but first you had to pay the factor a back-hander. It was £40; many of the people in that part of Glasgow got their inside toilets this way, by appealing directly to the housing factor's fervent corruption. It was the accepted method, and a woman who worked at the children's playgroup used to collect the guy's money. The go-between worked out what you wanted, found out what was available, and one day accepted a short ribbon of tenners over the milk-crate, with a wink and a smile. The keys would come soon after, and you were in. I can't really remember Bathgate Street, but it's a place planted firmly in my imagination. We lived there a very short time, and it was never very remarkable: a very straight and grey line, with continuous blocks opening sharp onto the street on both sides, with the odd hairdresser's shop, the odd dairy, quite close to the end, where a railway ran through a gully.

Allan and Mary McDonald, who lived in our flat at number 34 before us, went off to the new town of Cumbernauld, fit for a new life. Across the landing were the Conlons, Mrs Katie and Mr Charlie, who would keep an eye on us. The whole family must have looked liked children to them. They became a by-word, in later times, once we'd joined the McDonalds in fleeing to the New World, a by-word for good neighbourliness. They saw babies come, including me, and swapped flats with us – theirs was bigger and had coin-ops. The street twinkles very distantly in my memory, but it burns always brighter in my head. Like the city of before – the place of relatives whose lives are ill-apparent or gone – the Glasgow of the sixties I've drawn up has been drawn from the experience of others, the say-so of records and pictures and testimonies and plans. It is strange how the accounts will so often vary – no one, as I try to unlock these ways of life that conditioned my own, will wholly agree with another. It is right that way, of course. Others will have versions of their own.

The street was full of Strombolis and Strachans and Forresters and Bells. Georgie Forrester played with my eldest brother, Michael, in the street; they dodged cars (not always successfully: Georgie got hit once, and Michael had to run round to fetch Mrs Forrester at St Anne's, where she was no doubt praying for something like that never to happen). There might have been an ice-cream van in the street one day, and I might have walked towards it holding Michael's hand. There was wire blocking off the railway, you could see the half-built Whitevale flats where Michael and Georgie and one of the Ionta boys played, and the van gleamed up close, all fondant and white. A man with dark hair might have leant down with a cone, he might have stuck a chocolate flake in, and smiled. And he might never have been there at all.

My da was working as a joiner by then, my mum cleaned at a garage in the Gallowgate. In those streets, in that time, it seems there was a general way of life for men, and a quite separate way for women. The wife's life – encumbered and enlightened by demanding kids who'd consume their mummy's prime then judge her ever after – was seldom charmed or light or funny. The pubs held out to their men, offering an evening's chance at being somebody else, a bright and rowdy spell of boasting, of lively self-transportation, racing the pulse, soaking strife, and offering the promise of some tender oblivion. Women with kids could seldom take part in that. They waited at home, or at the homes of each other, 'nursing' – as I'd later learn from Robert Burns – 'their wrath to keep it warm'. And violence was a feature of many such homes. Women would get it, and some kids did too, if they opened their mouths at the close of the day. Whatever was happening at the Sorbonne in 1968, there were traditions in places like Glasgow, in many places besides, that went staggering on as before.

You might say that a certain amount of violence was accepted. And this was even more true of violence out in the street – organized violence – than of that taking place in people's homes. A sense of some gangsters as surrogate guardians of their home patch's welfare is still there today. It was common to feel that way, to see these little Caesars, these slashing bogeymen, these proto-Mafiosi, as ruthless hardmen, yes, but ones who had a certain concern for the values of the world they moved around in. The scarred king of the area around the Barrowland dancehall in those years was a man called James Kemp. He could be seen with his Crombie-coated footmen – one of whom was a relative of mine I'll call Ian – around the corners, doing his thing in lending and protection. Sometimes he'd appear at the door of the Barrowland, take out an open razor from an inside pocket, and slice off the tie of someone tall and handsome, waiting in line for a night at the dancing.

Everyone I spoke to called Kemp frightening but fair. As so often before, there was truth and there was folklore in people's whispered accounts of what went on. Kemp was often seen helping old women across the street with their laundry. Other times, he was signing his name on debtors' necks with a blade. One man, who in those days played football on Glasgow Green every Sunday, told me of time spent strenuously and deliberately missing goals, when playing against Kemp's team, for which Kemp stood as goalie. People still wince and shuffle and bare their lower teeth in disgust when talking about the area's most notorious clash between gang-leaders: a fight under the Barrowland, in amongst the market-stalls, between Kemp and Thompson, the Ice-cream warrior, a fight in which each man cut the other to ribbons.

Mr Kemp had a handicapped son who nobody ever saw, and

troubles that couldn't be solved in his usual ways. He started to come round to our house, asking my mum if he could take Michael, her first son, out for a walk. My brother, before I was born, had a head of blond curls and eyes fit to swim in. That's what they said, and that's what Kemp saw, no doubt, as he pushed his little friend around the Gallowgate in the afternoon. Everyone, my mother reminded herself, everyone knows that he could come to no harm in the company of James Kemp, and he never did. Kemp was good to him, and – as was his way – he made sure everybody else was good to him too. Michael would come back from his exciting journey around the Barras market with pockets weighed down with half-crowns – gifts from stall-holders and passers-by who may have been pleased to have the acquaintance of Jamesie's little boy.

In the much-altered city of the sixties, my parents, like most people parents or not, knew that Glasgow was a rough place. A lot of it was out of the way, some of it was mythical perhaps, but there was a feel, a certain knowledge pure and secure, that people could come to harm in no time at all if they didn't watch what they were doing. The details of the past were certainly obscure, the streets looked different, but some historical notions clung on, something remained, of past consortings with violence and extremity. It may, depending on who you were, have been there in your family; it may have been there in your street-as-it-used-to-be. Among many whose names had been round and about for a while, though, it may have been there in both family and place.

But where it wasn't in your own life – or in the previous lives of your own – it was probably just round in the next street. Or surrounding you. The widening, circular drama of city violence was something in which most people could play a small part. In the second half of the fifties, when my mother was working as a spooler at Templeton's Carpet Factory, just off the London Road, some murders were to take place which would always stick in her mind. They stayed, and took up room, because they skirted her life. That's the way of it: the killing of people, and people's disappearance, makes us aware of our being here, in a very specific place, and of the chance of our just as easily not being here at all, the chance that passed us by, the chance of not being. Murder at the heart of your community never leaves you.

Before it was a matter for the papers in 1958, the Denholm Bakery on London Road was the place where my mother went with her pals from the factory to buy their dinner. It had the fairly usual assortment of hot Scotch pies, bridies, sausage rolls, sandwiches, and cakes. It was run by a man called William Watt. His wife, who was an invalid, and their sixteen-year-old daughter, and Mrs Brown, his sister-in-law, were murdered in September 1956 by a man called Peter Manuel. They were all shot in the head while they slept, by the slick killer who wanted to be liked by those in Glasgow's criminal underworld. Manuel was a ten-times murderer, who boasted to Mr Watt of what he'd done, and made snide insiderish comments about the victims in pubs around the Gallowgate. He threw a Webley revolver, then a Beretta, into the Clyde under the Stockwell Bridge, and they were later recovered. They helped convict him for nine of the murders – the tenth, of a taxi driver in Newcastle, was beyond the jurisdiction of the Scottish courts. Manuel became the last person to be legally executed in Glasgow.

He was the sort of killer nobody could understand. He chose victims without motive, he killed without gain, he talked too much. He was almost all bad; though he might not have been psychotic. At his trial, the judge observed that he was 'very, very bad without being mad'. After his identity and his murderous activity was known, people in our part of Glasgow responded to these weird features in his character with amazement and disgust and no recognition. But they recognized the places in the plot – the buildings entered and left, the shops referred to, the pubs, some of the streets – and they heard the familiar ring in the accents of those giving evidence, and of him standing trial for his life. And my mother knew the face of Mr Watt, the man first accused; she'd often seen him with the women in his family. They'd exchanged words, perhaps, and passed money and packages hand to hand; they'd been in the same spaces; they had each been, if only fleetingly and not always consciously, a part of the other's experience of the city. And just there, with that and no more, in that powdery shop, my babyless mother, eighteen years of age, is frozen for me, quite stilled and unknowing, in the company of those whose lives would be taken from them.

Manuel's psychiatric reports were compiled when he was very young, when he was in approved school or Borstal or something. They were just out of the vaults; no one had been allowed to see them for years. I knew what his connection was to my history of absences: I had come to my point. Did I want to know anything more about Peter Manuel? I opened the file. Some facts came tumbling and I lifted my pencil. 'He attended the school at Our Lady of Good Aid in Motherwell.' 'Claims he got Communist tuition at Borstal,' 'Very obedient until 11 years old,' 'His father, an insurance agent,' 'Last June, had a nosebleed at Blackpool and took mental black out. Very nervous and violent temper. Has vivid imagination. Always seems tired and sleeps too much,' 'He spends his leisure time at pictures, dancing, and in public houses.' That was enough. Manuel could've killed anyone, he could have chosen my mother, he could have chosen anyone at all.

MY MOTHER TELLS me I was a quiet baby, easily shushed into silence by the front window at Bathgate Street. She'd pull back the Terylene, loosen the white netting, and there the world would be. Perhaps the ruinous storms of May lingered on. I couldn't see to tell, I couldn't sniff the air. Often as my mother looked down at the street, she'd see a man walking home from work, a man who lived in a flat on the other side of the street. He looked a bit like my father. But his hair was neatly combed, he wore a tie and a clean mackintosh. A tie, a mackintosh, and he held onto a briefcase. He swung it by his side as he walked, whistling. He was very smart, this man, and he looked after his family as well as himself. His name was William – William McDowell – and he looked as well and as happy as anyone would who so clearly did the right things. McDowell was a good man, wasn't he good? My mother would see him from the window, sometimes with his wife – Rosemary or something – and they'd look healthy and nice all the time. Several years later, when we'd escaped to the new world, to a New Town in Ayrshire, McDowell's face would look out from the front of newspapers. His mistress would go missing in the company of her baby boy Andrew. They would never be found. Beyond our curtains at Bathgate Street, outside the window, striding against the wet, was the whistling, whistling Mr McDowell.

My granda Beef was dead by 1968, and his widow, my granny Doc, was beginning to get her life back together. She was the eldest of the ten children bred by Famie Dunn, the hawker I wrote about before who lived up the Gallowgate. Agnes Kelly Dunn Docherty, my maternal granny, was always the life-and-soul. In most respects, she was a kind of opposite to my other granny: she wasn't one much for the chapel; she was all for dancing, mad for singing, and peroxide, and would soon be off on the newish package holidays to Spain. They were both generous; they each possessed a different sort of dignity; and each was as stuck in their way as the other. 'I don't go out much,' my granny Doc used to say, clip-on earrings and fake fur ashimmer, 'just Tuesdays, Wednesdays, Thursdays, Fridays, and Saturdays.' She was an entertainer, a dresser-up, a Glesga chanteuse – as devoted to the good life as my other sweet granny was to the spiritual one. 'Nae point sittin' aboot mopin' an' greetin',' she'd toot, pouring you out an underage tumbler of lager.

In my earliest days my granny would be at my mother to get out and have more of a life. My mum had stopped going to the dancing when she got married in 1959. The old Barrowland, the one founded by Margaret McIver before the war, had burned down the year before the marriage, and old Maggie died in that year too. With a half-joking smirk, my mother used to say that she'd never have got married if that hadn't happened. With some of her teenage pals, she stood in the Gallowgate on the night of the fire, and they watched the place burn down. Many of them turned away in tears, knowing something was finally over. They drifted off and got married, and some went away from the city altogether. But the dancehall reopened on Christmas Eve 1960, with a different look, some newer neon, a licence to sell drink, and a crowd more suited to the times. It had always been a big-band place: two thousand people danced there on a good night, and the numbers reached their peak just after the war, when they sectioned off a part of the hall for jivers. The original band, Billy Blue and the Bluebirds, gave way, at the toll of the fifties, to a new band formed and fronted by one of their number: Billy McGregor (with his Gaybirds). At the very centre of the Calton, the dancehall spun through the years, glistening like a mirror-ball. But there was change, inside the hall as out in the city itself, and the second Barrowland, by 1968, was wowing them a little less glitzily. The main room had a smaller, woozier band, and in the other room they played records. My granny Doc and her two married daughters went to the Thursday night 'over-25s'. Not every week, but now and then, it offered the chance of a night away from their families and routine hassles. Faces would bob through these rooms, laughing under the lights, caring for nothing, looking almost familiar.

The Albert, the Locarno, the Plaza, the Majestic, the Barrowland. Each of the big Glasgow dancehalls had stories about them, all of them had dramas, and each had a reputation of one sort or another. The Barrowland was the most notorious of all, standing as it did as a shimmering axis, an oily pivot, around which the Calton community had for ever seemed to turn. But it was the central spot for many who lived in other bits of the city, too. The Thursday Night had a reputation for drawing a good crowd: the older sort who'd seldom go out, the sort with husbands and wives left at home, the sort tied down, with kids and that. Some were just out for a jaunt with sisters and friends and perhaps mothers if they were game. But many would be AWOL from home, slipping their wedding rings off at the door.

Patricia Docker worked as an auxiliary nurse at Mearnskirk

Hospital. She had a job-share with her mother, working the night shift Friday to Monday. She'd split from her husband, who was with the RAF in Lincolnshire, and lived now with her mum and dad at a house on Langside Place in Battlefield. On the evening of Thursday 22 February, wearing a yellow woollen dress, brown shoes, and a duffle coat, and carrying a brown handbag, she left her four-year-old son in the care of her dad, John Wilson, and went off for a night out at the Majestic ballroom in Hope Street. On the way into town, she must have changed her mind, for she ended up at the Barrowland. The rest of the evening is a blank. Patricia's body was discovered near her home early next morning by a man called Maurice Goodman, who found her battered and dead at the door of his garage in Carmichael Lane. She had been strangled with something like a leather belt. Lying near her body was a used sanitary pad.

Many who were at the Barrowland on these Thursday Nights were not really there. That's what they'd say; that was the sort of night it was. Police trying to establish a victim's movements in such an open space could usually rely on cumulative sightings, admissions, and bits of talk. But no one would talk. A lot of those who were at the dancehall would not step forward, they couldn't speak, they were never supposed to have been there in the first place. Wives without husbands, husbands away from wives, they were all supposed to be somewhere else. For some, more than some, it was a place you went to in order to lose something of your identity: few, especially among the men, were keen to step forward and reveal themselves. Everything went quiet.

Police searched the River Cart, trying to recover Pat's clothes and handbag, all of which were missing. Did she take taxis, or walk, or dance, visit the Ladies, buy a drink, put in her coat? Come on. One person came forward. Our witness may have spotted Patricia Docker very briefly, waiting at the entrance to Queen's Park, on Langside Avenue, just after eleven that night. She'd looked like someone waiting for a bus. A Morris 1000 Traveller stopped in front of her; she may have got in. It was difficult to see in the dark. But you could see it was a Morris? It's difficult. When police started speaking from the bandstand, asking for help, and walking through the crowd in plain clothes, many of the Barrowland's punters, for a wee while at least, felt that their cover had been blown. Nights like that were about secrecy, and you couldn't be doing with the fuzz turning up on your door on a Sunday afternoon, quizzing you in front of the kids about nights spent at dancehalls. Places you'd never gone into; dances danced with partners you'd never dream of.

Mackeith Street lies just on the other side of the London Road from the Calton, over by Bridgeton Cross. When I was one or two, Mackeith Street was being demolished. A lot of the tenements stood empty, 'condemned property', as people still say. Jemima McDonald lived at number 15, with her children Elisabeth (twelve), Andrew (nine) and Alan (seven). Her husband was nowhere to be seen. Eighteen months after the murder of Pat Docker, the Barrowland was thriving again, the police long since having given up. It was a warm Saturday, 16 August 1969, when Jemima went off to the Barrowland, leaving the kids safe with her sister Margaret, who lived across the landing. It was a nice night outside.

It's not like her, thought Margaret, when Jemima failed to come back that night. The next day, the kids were all out on the street; it was scorching. As usual, in their own gangs, they'd climb in and out of the derelict buildings, hitting and adventuring. Some neighbours heard a group of children, in the afternoon, talking among themselves about 'a body in the building'. That's the sort of thing kids say, excited on hot afternoons. But by the next morning Margaret was beginning to panic: where the hell is she? Hardly able to think, she walked down through the empty buildings, through the rooms at number 23, and there she found her sister's body. She'd been strangled, some of her things were missing. Margaret ran for the police. At first, they didn't connect it with the death of Pat Docker. But they looked again. She'd been strangled with tights, she'd been at the Barrowland, her handbag was missing, and – surely a coincidence? – she was having her period at the time.

Detectives made an announcement at the Barrowland, asking for people to come forward, and promising that 'domestic problems of witnesses would be respected'. As the dancers stood still, police projected a picture of Jemima McDonald onto a screen and issued a full description. They looked at each other, and fell quiet. A woman thought she had seen the girl on the screen. She saw her sitting on a couch last Saturday night with a man. He had sandy-coloured short hair, was tall, wearing a really white shirt. A boy reported seeing a couple just like that, sitting in a pub nearby, and he gave a description that matched some of the girl's detail. The hunt became intense. A tutor at Glasgow School of Art interviewed the two witnesses and drew up a graphic impression of the suspect, a drawing which met their idea of him, and it was quickly circulated to newspapers. It was pasted up in the streets all around. But nothing. Everyone was talking about it, but no one talking to the police was able to offer much guidance. After a while, the management of the dancehall pulled the plug on police activity. 'That's enough,' they said, 'we're losing all our customers.'

An Identikit picture is a curious thing: a picture made up from features that may appear on a mass of different faces; a nose that one might have, eyes from somebody else, a hairstyle you see all the time, lips you once noticed on a film star. Bits from all over the place, coming together to catch a killer. We imagine we know this killer's face, and we make him up from bits of other people. Until the killer is caught, every man in the area who shares one or two of those facial bits – those bumps and clefts and lines and styles – will fall under some suspicion. The artist's drawing of the Barrowland's invisible killer would soon give way to an Identikit, and the whole city would begin to think seriously of how they might be living in the company of a killer. In these years, when Glasgow was pulling and hauling to get away from its past, they were also looking over their shoulder to see bits of a killer on the faces of passers-by. A community living with an uncaught serial killer is a place where many feel under threat, and many under suspicion. Long after the murders seem to have stopped, killers stay on in the minds of those who lived, and feared a brutal end to life, under their dark spell. This happens with all killers, but much more so with ones who are never caught: they can always kill again. Their power remains, never revealed, never dispelled. You can live long in such a community. The murderer, having no known identity, takes little parts from the identities of everyone. For ever Identikit, except to the good eye-witness, who knows of a singular face, and might – just might – clear the way to the murderer's door.

Helen was twenty-nine, and married to a soldier. He didn't mind her going out on a Thursday, he thought it funny that she still wanted to dance, and he'd babysit their two children to let her out. This night, her sister Jeannie came round wrapped in a green coat. There was an October freeze on. They left the house around 8.30 p.m., Helen throwing an imitation ocelot fur coat over her black dress, and grabbing her bag. Helen's house was in Earl Street, in Scotstoun, over by the city's West End, snug against the Clyde and the shipyards. They caught a bus going into town, and they jumped off at Glasgow Cross. It was busy around this time, and mist hung around the tops of the buildings. The two sisters began to walk up the Gallowgate, stopping here and there, to look into shops. They checked the sizes and prices of heels in the window of Gordon's Shoe Shop, at number 64, and wandered on, past Lynch's pub (174), pausing a second at Bayne & Ducket (176), and striding on, arm in arm, past the City Ham and Egg Stores (208), slowing down near Burns's pawnshop (215) and here turning into Kent Street. They went down to the Traders' Tavern, which was rowdy and full, and met their pals Marion Cadder and Jean O'Donnell. They chatted together and gossiped, the four of them, and drank a few whiskies each. The air was full of laughing and arguing and blue with fag smoke; the beer-mats were sodden with spilt drink.

Just after ten, the pub shut, and they walked down to the Barrowland. Couples, and groups of women, were already dancing in the main hall. The girls split up quite quickly. A man called John asked Jeannie to dance (they're all called John, she thought). This one was a roofer, from Castlemilk. He could dance pretty well, pretty steadily, and he wasn't much the worse for drink. Helen stood at the side watching and smoking a cigarette. Sometimes watching was all right, just to stand and listen to the music. That was all right, you could feel quite peaceful doing that, quite content, just watching everybody else. A tall man came up to her. She was happy to dance with him, she seemed to like him, and they stayed by each other, dancing and talking, for the rest of the night. Jeannie and John stayed nearby, sometimes coming over to exchange jokes or drinks. 'Helen, this is John.' 'Jeannie, this is John.' They laughed, and the men sniffed and looked sheepish, sipping their pints and looking around. With regard to each other, the two Johns barely exchanged glances, never mind words.

'He wasn't the Barrowland type,' Jeannie said later of Helen's partner. 'Many of those who used to go were kind of rough or drunk. But he was nice, very nice, quite polite and well spoken.' Jeannie was the witness. She would become the only person who had really looked at him, and when thinking back to those looks, knew them to be the looks of the man who must have murdered her young sister. For her, he had only one identity, one face, and no Identikit – however well they'd compose it from her suggestions – would match her knowledge of him. He was 5' 10" or so; he had nice eyes; he looked reserved and well turned out; his suit was brown, well cut, with three buttons; his shirt was clean, light blue; his tie was striped; his skin was clear and fresh; his front two teeth overlapped; his hair was sandy and cropped unfashionably short, rounded at the back; he wore short suede boots, not shoes. She saw a watch on his right wrist, one of those ones with an interlacing leather strap. This man John was somewhere between, say, twenty-five and thirty-five. But there were things lost to our witness, details that wouldn't come back: he'd mentioned his surname – what was it? – Templeton, Sempleson, Emerson, or something.

The music stopped, and they moved downstairs to get their coats. He wasn't the regular sort, Jeannie thought again. He just wasn't . . . well, there was something unusual about him, something unexpected. He was the sort of guy you'd see, but not often at the dancing. That was the thing: look at the fastidious way he smoothed down his scarf before putting on his coat. He spoke with a west coast accent, probably Glasgow, only more refined. Jeannie put some money into the cigarette machine, and pulled the lever for Embassy Tipped. It was stuck. She tried a few times before Helen's John got angry, demanding the manager and assuring her that he would sort it out. The manager appeared, in the company of a bruiser, and explained that these things happened. John berated him, and the establishment, demanding recompense, enquiring who the local MP was. Helen tried to apologize for the fuss. An assistant manager coughed up the twenty pence.

On the way out, John, firmly but quietly, was laying into the manager and his crummy dancehall. 'My father says these places are dens of iniquity,' he said. 'They set fire to this place to get the insurance money and done it up with the money they got.' Jeannie walked down the Gallowgate with the roofer from Castlemilk, and Helen walked at the back with her John. She could hear her laughing; Helen made out she was amazed at something she was being shown. Jeannie turned round, and saw that he was flashing what appeared to be an ID card, or membership card. They arrived at the taxi rank beside Lawsons, on the London Road side of Glasgow Cross. The rank here is always busy. It sits under an old bit of iron bridge – a damp patch, always murky and dripping with rainwater. The roofer said goodbye, he was going to George Square for the late bus home. While the other John looked away, Jeannie got up to Helen's ear. 'Is he seeing us home?' she asked. 'Where does he live?' Helen just smiled and waved her hand to nowhere.

The three of them got into a black cab, which made off down Argyle Street, going west, through the lights of the city centre. They talked about the past summer; Jeannie and Helen had gone to the coast, to the new town of Irvine, in Ayrshire, where they'd a caravan. The conversation was a bit slow: John seemed to resent Jeannie having stuck around. But the mention of Ayrshire got him talking about golf. Someone he knew, someone in his family, had recently got a hole in one. The cab passed Lewis's, and went under the bridge at Central Station. John then muttered something about adulterous women; about religion, Celtic and Rangers. 'I don't drink at Hogmanay,' he said, 'I pray.' He was going all into himself; Helen was amused by the way he took out some cigarettes, gave her one, then put them away, neither taking one himself nor offering one to Jeannie. Jeannie asked if she couldn't have one, then took three for badness. He looked out of the window on his side as they passed Monkland Street. An advertising hoarding stood out as they rumbled past: 'After work you need a GUINNESS' it said. Out of Jeannie's side, a little newsagent flashed past; its lights were still on, and billboards for the *Evening Times* remained outside, behind metal grilles. She took little of it in. But the billboards they passed, had they not seen them already, were advertising that evening's paper – the late final for Thursday 30 October 1969. The headline was large and bold: SEX MANIAC SENT TO CARSTAIRS. The news itself was somewhere else by then, abandoned on train seats, stuffed in bins, and lying around living-room sofas all over the city. 'Glasgow sex maniac James Ferguson', the story said, 'left the dock in the High Court in Edinburgh in tears today after being ordered to be detained in the state institution at Carstairs without limit of time.' As the cab rolled towards Kingston sometime after twelve, that news lay somewhere back in the past. It meant nothing to them, though it may mean something to us.

They passed the area where the new Kingston Bridge was nearing completion. Mounds of earth and rubble lay on every side; concrete blocks spanned the Clyde, half done, with metal rods dangling over the top like frizz. John seemed to recognize this part of town: he said something obscure about foster children, and how that was OK, Moses had been fostered. They passed some high flats. Yes, he recognized it, his father and somebody else had worked there, before the flats. He stared out of the window; and they spoke on and off until the cab approached Earl Street. John insisted that Jeannie be dropped off first, she lived further on, in Kelso Street. Jeannie told them just to drop her at a roundabout nearby. Helen waved to her out of the back window as the car spun round. Jeannie waved back, and yawned, as the cab rumbled away to quietness.

The night-service bus on Dumbarton Road picked a man up around 2 a.m. He didn't look right. A passenger noticed the man's jacket was muddy, and he had what appeared to be a fresh scratch on his face, just under the eye. He looked agitated. But the passenger didn't look much closer, he didn't think much about it, and the guy got off the bus just past Gray Street. The man who disappeared from the late bus, and into Glasgow's dark, also disappeared at that point into Glasgow mythology. He'd never be seen again, not as a murderer, though he'd just left Helen Puttock in a back-court at 95 Earl Street, strangled to death, naked, and with a used sanitary towel placed under her left armpit. The Barrowland dancehall, and the area that turned around it, had known violence and murder before this, but they'd never found its culprits this elusive, the crimes this pointless and open to multiple interpretation. The whole city felt the weight of these crimes. They were different. The killer must have been part of their community, but he was missing from it, leaving them only to contemplate the community itself.

My mother always told me she recognized that made-up face of Bible John. She knew it, she just did: she'd met that man. And so did every second mother who'd been in that world at the time. When I was older, I found that my friends who'd been born in Glasgow would know the name Bible John, and their mothers too would recognize his image. The Scottish tabloids bring him back from time to time, knowing, as I think I do myself, that his mystery, for many, is bound up now with the mysteries of an era in Glasgow. Many were more than usually touched by those terrible murders. Perhaps they know that the victims could have been any of them, and the murderer... Well, the murderer is missing, and there's no telling who he was, or wasn't.

This was the situation in the first two years of my life. Our world was being turned upside-down in the search for a man who nobody knew, but who everybody knew a bit. It was a Glasgow problem, this one, and little bits of Glasgow history had been embedded in the story, just as they had been in the dark combustions of the past. Every barber shop, every dentist, every religious grouping, every tailor's, every institution with membership cards, every dancehall, every golf club, every ship, every household containing men with overlapping teeth, or light hair, or a club tie, or smoking Embassy Tipped, or whatever. The drama was horrible and sad, and it was for everyone, more or less. It was the biggest and most intensive manhunt in Scotland's criminal history. Everyone saw Bible John somewhere, and rang the police. He was on a bus, he's outside Marks & Spencers, he's in the Horseshoe Bar, he works at the Kelvingrove Art Gallery. Some sandy-haired trouser-presser strolling through the Calton would be stopped, or grabbed, or arrested, under suspicion of being the city's most notorious killer. The city police eventually gave out cards saying *I am certified as not being Bible John* to men with a certain look, such was the grief those men suffered. But still their identity was doubted. Hugh Cochrane presented a troubling documentary on the killings for the BBC at the beginning of the seventies, ending the programme with a quotation from Jeremiah, 23: 24. 'Can any hide himself in secret places, that I shall not see him? saith the Lord.'

IN 1994, I went back to the abandoned Marine. A stone building much like an old-fashioned school, it stands in Anderson Street, in Partick, not far from the home Helen Puttock kept with her husband and two kids. After her death, this site (the home of the riverside police, known as the Marine Division) became the headquarters for the whole investigation. Dozens of police followed thousands of leads: conducting interviews, checking manual records and reported sightings. They endlessly sifted data, more and more of it every day; combing through the details of the city's population, eliminating some, homing in on others, all in the hope of finding the one name that would match what they knew of this disappeared killer. They never found the name.

The place was now empty, the windows boarded up. The stairs had chunks of plaster lying on them, there were holes in the walls, there were glue cans lying here and there. Some offices still had sticks of furniture in them, and shelves. And in the main room, once the incident room in this search for Bible John, there was little to tell of, just a tin kettle against the far wall with its element ripped out. I tried to think of how many names you'd have to sift, and how many times, to be sure your killer wasn't just walking around the next corner as before. Then I went downstairs to see the cells. They were small, these cells, with names cut into the tiles on all sides. Standing on a stool, I could see through a square grille at the top of the far wall. I put my eyes up to it, and took in a slanted bit of modern Glasgow.

THIN AYRSHIRE

DAVID GIBSON WAS a man stiff and parsonical; by all accounts the sort of man who got things done. You could say he was obsessed with ridding Glasgow of its slums, of turning them into something bright and high and unquestionably modern. That's what he wanted, and he'd already made vast advances towards getting it when he became Convener of Glasgow Corporation's housing committee in 1964, a post he wasn't to hold for long. We're fond of hating his ideas nowadays, of seeing the horror of those damp flats and pointing up the stupidity of the planning. But Gibson and his allies were visionaries of a sort. They thought they could obliterate the past with new production, and they had reason to think a project like that might turn out to be for the good of everybody. It may be obvious now how wrong they were, but Gibson's urge to remake, to deliver his own people out of the slums and into a pure new shock world, has plenty of wrong-headed nobility in it, and no shortage of high-mindedness.

Gibson was a workaholic. He was the most frighteningly determined house builder of his age, and he made time for little else. When not forging political alliances, steam-rollering committees with his rhetoric, with his guile, and not out searching the city for gap-sites where he might build more blocks, Gibson would put in some hours at his wife's sub-post office in Springfield Road. He smoked furiously, and drank sugary tea like there was no tomorrow. He'd search the city in his car late at night, after office hours, looking for possible construction sites. He hardly ever ate. He was agitated, burning on all cylinders, and he died in 1964. A colleague in Motherwell later described him as the man who killed himself trying to solve Glasgow's housing problem.

He solved it well enough, if only for the shortest time. Those blocks couldn't handle the Glasgow weather, and people couldn't live on top of one another and still feel they were in a community. Dampness spread, violence brewed, lifts broke down, vandals got to work. I was hardly into my twenties when many of Gibson's blocks were being evacuated or blown down. His dream had been an accelerated version of the dreams of other people, most of whom just wanted an inside toilet. But his dream palaces were coming down, bit by bit, in ways too intimate to be staved off in a flurry of blame. Gibson had wanted housing for Glaswegians within the city itself; there were others who felt the answer lay elsewhere. The elect of Edinburgh and London had been thinking about new towns, and they were of a mind to decant as many of Glasgow's young families as would happily go. East Kilbride, Cumbernauld, Livingston, Glenrothes, and Irvine. These were the Scottish New Towns, all designated by 1968. For many, they seem to have represented the New World.

THINGS HAD GROWN cumbersome in Bathgate Street. A certain chapter in my parents' lives – youth, I suppose – was over, and they wanted something brighter and greener and breezier for the future. They wanted something better than what the city they'd grown up in could offer us. My da was always on the look out for a big idea, and one came to him in 1970 when he was doing some joinery work in the Ayrshire town of Kilwinning. He was vaguely familiar with the area, it was only twenty-five miles outside the city, and it was part of this new-town development at Irvine. Of all the Scottish New Towns, this one seemed the least suburban, the most out on its own. It was on the coast, so there was the sea; it was surrounded by fields, so there was all this green; and the houses were big – no one had lived or died in those new houses, and the whole community seemed to be growing out of the ground fully formed. Altogether that day, as he did his ceiling work and looked around him from the scaffold, he must have looked on something that seemed like fertile soil on which to plant a new life for him and his wife and his kids. A fresh start was required, and this was the big idea. Glasgow was rough, dark. This was ventilated and open. He brought the good news back to Bathgate Street that night.

My ma knew it was near to Saltcoats, a west coast summer resort full of cinemas and cafes, a beach place, where they used to go on holiday as kids. Everybody in Glasgow knew Saltcoats; like Rothesay and Largs, it was one of those promenaded seaside towns with signatured pink rock and dirty postcards and sand in the sandwiches. Summer trains from Glasgow Central Station to Saltcoats were called Breezers, and the coast was long associated with fresh air and sunshine and good health. The idea that people would come to Saltcoats for their holidays would crack us up in later years. It would always come up when kids were moaning on about essential school trips to the Algarve, this bit about Breezers and holidays to Saltcoats from the grimy city. To us it was a scream, the ultimate in fuddy-duddyism, but that was later. We grew up there, and for us it was the city that was fascinating and mysterious. The beach was, well, the beach was just buckets of sand.

That's the sort of thing we might say, and we might even have believed it too, but now that I think of it, and of how we actually spent our time around the beach, I know we must have known better. Our heads were full of sea-things. We were wee salt-sea experts as we gadded about the front, in and out of rock pools, under harbours and piers, among the boats, absconding after breakfast, stowing away till it was time for your tea. Someone said to me the other day that there was, of course, no such thing as a hot day in Scotland. I remember very differently, and some of these days around our new sea-world were extremely hot. There was one such day on the beach at Seamill, a little way up the coast. It was roasting, so it was. I was sunburnt, and was skipping in and out of a pool of water coming from a pipe on the grassy bank. Our blanket was spread out in the sand just beside that. I had stripy trunks on; my brothers were playing at burying each other in the sand up to the neck, and my mum was fiddling with Tupperware bowls. I ran the long way to the water's edge and saw my dad there with his brown pin-stripe trousers rolled up just past the ankle. (I later found out he couldn't swim. But he never wore things like shorts anyway. I've never actually seen his legs in my life.) Other people were splashing about and I sat in at the edge, letting waves come over me, but keeping my head out of the water by propping myself up on my elbows. My da looked over now and then. I stared out past where people were swimming and splashing; you could see clear bumps in the distance. Irelands. Islands. I could taste salt in my mouth; my elbows were sinking in. I sat up and watched the sea and the sunniness shining off it. It was great, and very beautiful. My da came over and stood me up, and he pointed out to where the islands were. I knew the long one was called Arran and the boulder, the smaller one, was called Ailsa Craig. He wiped my mouth, and pointed out again. There were dark shapes away out, between us and Arran, and I thought they were sharks. He laughed, and screwed a fag stub into the sand. 'Submarines,' he said, 'subs.'

The housing developments of Irvine New Town seemed, to our first eyes, like places with nothing missing. We looked on them as places with no past, with no secrets or dark configurations under their sunny tops. It was 1970, and we felt kind of like the first men to walk on the moon. There was a children's play-area in the middle of each square; little clusters of rock and bench and swing, surrounded by triangular patches of bush and mucky flower-bed. Man-made grass slopes rose there too, bordered by kerb and a car park marked out with paint. Those rocks and slopes, for many of us, were our first domain, and they'd prove themselves equal to representing the entire universe, and no less. The way to the other squares in the scheme was through what we called tunnels but were actually spaces between houses which worked like underpasses, because in each case a bedroom of one house would run over the top of the gap. You could also move along a number of narrow paths made from gaps behind the gardens, and as a child, you always had the feeling you were in some sort of clever maze, some complicated underworld designed as much for amusement as for function. The prefabricated world of that housing scheme, Pennyburn, still sits in my head like something invented only this morning. You could blindfold me, and take me back, and I'd find my way from one end to the other without too much trouble. Except that I wouldn't, of course, seeing as much of it has changed by now, just as you'd expect.

In what the scheme's builders liked to call Phase One, there were thirty families in each square, four squares in each block, and four blocks in the whole grid. There were two roads into it – Cranberry Road and Muirside Road – and these came off a main artery that circled the scheme and ran down towards the old town of Kilwinning and the rest of the world. The concept of the 'old town' wasn't known to me till later, as those first days were spent blissfully exploring the scheme, and the little by-ways and borders that constituted its outer rim. If you went through the tunnel at the east of our square you came to a field, fenced off and marshy, with the playing-fields of St Michael's Academy opening up on the other side of it. In the middle of the field there stood an electricity generating thing, painted green, and surrounded by a spiked metal fence. I think there was a hut beside it, with a padlock on the door, and a giant television mast above it, which must have stretched up to fifty feet in the air, though to my tilted head in those days it seemed to stretch all the way into the clouds. To me, it was a giant beanstalk sort of thing.

At the bottom end of this field, forming a corner with the playing-fields, the railway line, and the flats, there was a bridge which I remember first being made of rickety wood and later of iron and wire. This led to some open land, to MacDonald's farm and an old abandoned farmhouse called Cranberry Moss (which later became our community centre). But mainly it led to the shops underneath the flats, and to Pennyburn Primary

School just beyond that. As I say, when we first arrived, there was all sorts of digging and building going on there (and there would be for years to come, as all this farmyard and field would eventually be turned into more housing). The shops by the bridge were finished, I'm sure, but they didn't all have tenants in them as yet. Or maybe they did. There was Mario's Chip Shop (run by a gay Scottish-Italian sophisticate who would soon employ my mother); Terry's DIY (owned by Terry and his Chinese wife; the business only boomed until all the inhabited houses were done, then he moved out to make way for a bookie). Then there was Preston's Newsagent (Mr and Mrs Preston, hard nosed, thin lipped, from somewhere in England, with jars of sweeties to the ceiling). It starts to fade out a bit from there. I know there was a supermarket called something like Centra, but the first owners hated kids and were always throwing us out. They went away quite soon, that family, and an Indian family took it over. Right enough: the next few units were the last ones, and they were taken up by the New Penny Bar, which was at one time run by a ferocious character called Jack. A bunch of mothers in our square – May, Liz, Mary, Gina, and my own mum – got part-time jobs cleaning the local primary school which sat next to the New Penny. Some of the young women worked at more than one part-time job. My mum went out sometimes in the evenings, to work at a place called Wonderloaf. This was the world, so far as I was concerned, until I was five or so years old. Each day would start with the noise of seagulls outside the window, our bunkbeds would rock a little, and the day would go ahead as if every second of it were unusual.

IRVINE NEW TOWN seemed all new at first; the ongoing construction – and the self-containing pattern of squares and tunnels and bridges and fields – made it seem, to a small child at least, as if nothing had been there before. The world of before, we imagined, was all just salt air and emptiness. Up until a certain age, of course, all children see their world as new. But we recognized that ours had been built specially for us, whatever lay beyond was out of bounds, beyond our ken. Everything we needed, everything we knew, was right there in concrete and chipboard. I presume there are things, separate things, which become linked in the mind of a child, and stay linked in the mind of the adult who grows out of some things but not of others. My childhood was about seeing things emerge out of nowhere, seeing buildings go up every day, as we played among the cement mixers, and seeing history come out of the blue, as we adventured, with increasing awareness, among the historical ruins in the towns and parks beyond our estate. As time went on, we wandered, too, into ruins of another sort; the empty factories and halted industries which surrounded us suddenly became central to our sense of where we lived, and how we lived. And, yes, of how they'd lived before we were thought of. We started to read books, some of us, and got to know properly the ancient ground under our stomping feet. Like I say, some things become linked in the minds of children: just as my sense of the family's history had been a wee bit dark and tied to thoughts of my missing relatives, so, too, was my sense of things emerging in our new town tied to the fact that people could disappear around us at the same time. As everything was coming, on all sides coming, so were things going, vanishing. The news of that, the feel of it, surrounded me then, or at least surrounded me in my own head. Sometimes it surrounds me still.

In those days, we had a budgie in the electrical cupboard called Joey. It would trill away in its cage, in the dark, and one day it just went quiet. It sounds daft, but for ages I thought I'd killed him. I remember trying to feed him a bit of McCowans Highland Toffee through the bars of his cage and him nibbling the end of it. I knew that budgies weren't to eat sweeties, but I fed it to him all the same. This was probably months before he dropped off, but it stuck in my mind. Dumb bird, I thought, shouldn't have swallowed it. Around the same time, one of my brothers came into the house talking about Father Burke, who was the parish priest at St Winnin's. He was dead in a coffin. The lid was off. (I could hear my brother saying it. It was dark outside, a Wednesday night.) What's that? He's green. Father Burke was Irish, he was green, he was in his coffin, dead. The lid was off, and everybody got to look in, or walk past and look in, or just walk past.

I had such a good time in the house. There's a period between being a toddler and being of school age that I remember well. I must have been about three or four because my brother Charlie was at school then, and he was only two years ahead of me. I was shy, always hiding in presses and behind a giant bottle-green sofa we had in the living-room that seemed like an entire planet to me. I was always finding coins and strange crumbs down the back of it. Bits of biscuit. Those afternoons with my mother smell of furniture polish and sound like a Hoover. My mum has always been a champion housekeeper; at that age, and for a while after, I thought she only had one hand, the left one. The other arm always ended in a clump of wet cloth, which she would draw over everything from the kitchen floor to her housebound son's jammy face (and usually all in one sweep). She would wipe my face, and sit me down in front of the telly, with a bowl of my favourite thing, which at that time was Ambrosia Creamed Rice, out of a tin. There was a giant vase of imitation flowers on top of the TV – some were shaped like sausages, with red glitter over them – and this arrangement my mum was always fussing over, always primping and fixing. I can't see the TV, is all I'd think. But you could watch it through her legs or squeezed round the side. There were two very important programmes on TV then, and they were programmes, I'm sure, which told me everything I cared to know about the world outside. The first, and favourite, was called *Mr Benn*. It was an animated show about a man who walked down a street and then went into a shop. Inside the shop he would go into the changing-room and be anyone and anywhere he liked. The second was brilliant too. It was called *Mary, Mungo and Midge*, and featured a group of pals (human and non-human) who lived in a block of flats; they would go up to the top in an elevator at the beginning of each show. I was sure the whole world was just like that.

I remember footering about in the coat press one day – the Hoover scraping away on the landing above me – and finding pens and bottles under all the coats. It was my thing to draw on the walls whenever I got the chance, and with a black marker I started drawing circles on the wall, big then wee, trailing away into the distance, getting smaller and smaller until they were just tiny black dots and then nothing at all. My dad was home, and I came out and met him in the hall. 'See this,' he said. Mick, Gerry and Charlie were standing out the back garden, my mother came down and started laughing, as we looked at the tree. 'See the apples have grown?' said my dad, laughing too. I was amazed, looking at this tree that went no higher than the kitchen window, amazed to see little red apples hanging from the branches. They were tiny, I thought, too wee for apples. They were Sellotaped on, and everybody laughed. It was a funny day, and we all laughed, and everything was fine. We had rocks in our garden, different coloured ones, that had been brought from the shore at Portencross. A circle of them surrounded the bottom of the v-shaped tree, the tree that couldn't grow apples on its own. I sat on half of the step – it was warm on my legs – drawing shapes on the other half with an orange rock.

Christmas 1973 was another good time. Michael got an ITT tape-recorder, the first one I'd ever seen. It was flat and wide, with a green button which would light up and say 'Batt OK' if you pressed it when the power was up. He got a Billy Connolly live tape; it was full of dirty jokes and was called, I think, *Raw Meat for the Balcony*. I would hear Michael and Gerry listening to it in their room at night, laughing their heads off. Christmas Day, in our house at least, always circulated around the telly. *Top of the Pops* was on, everybody was dancing on it, many of them wearing silver boots and things in their hair. Slade and Gary Glitter were the ones that year (Gerry and Mick preferred David Bowie and Roxy Music), and we sang and spoke into the tape-recorder. Charlie sang like Glitter; Michael came on and wished everybody a happy new year; Gerry came on and said he'd got everything he wanted; my da came on and said my mum was too drunk to speak, then she came on saying hi she was thirty-two. I came on sounding a bit wary, saying my name was Andrew and I was five. My mum was coaxing me from the side.

You had the feeling that family was important, maybe even that family was all there was, but you guessed there might be more to it than that. Whatever else, it was a rare day. My

73

pyjamas were made of navy blue nylon, and they had red borders round the wrists and collar. I didn't take them off all day, and at night, before climbing up to bed, I shone my new torch through the window, across the square, to Fergus, my pal in number 30. It was a knowing flash: it spoke of new excitements to come, of hopes that we'd soon be free to explore the world beyond our own houses, and even our own scheme. He flashed back. I think he knew that too, waving his torch from side to side in the dark. His torch flashed in celebration of a good day over, and in anticipation of better days to come.

One day, my mum took me into Irvine town centre in the afternoon. Kilwinning is a satellite of Irvine, the main town, as Pennyburn is a satellite of Kilwinning. We came from the station, and she brought me up to some high flats. My eyes were everywhere; the present wasn't just opening up in the usual way, it was suddenly opening up against the past. There were things around us that were old. All of a sudden, not everything was new. We went up in the elevator, and went into the flat of a woman who I'm sure was doing hair. My mum sat on a stool, I seem to remember, and she had a purple cap on her head with holes in it. Bits of hair had come through the holes. Yes, I'm sure it was a hairdressing day. I sat eating biscuits by the window. As you looked down at the river, you could see that they were demolishing an old bridge. There were diggers pulling and hauling, men in white helmets climbing over steel girders, right in the shadow of a great steeple. The church was fancy, the steeple went very high. I thought only television masts went as high as that.

THE FOUR-ARCH BRIDGE across the River Irvine was built

by a certain Thomas Brown in 1750, for the price of £350. Ten years before, the Royal Burgh's sunken wells, dank and rotten, had been replaced by the council. Pump wells were installed, and fresh water was all the rage. The second half of the eighteenth century, in a small Scottish market town like Irvine, was the period of great change. These years saw such towns evolving and changing at great speed; from isolated rural villages full of peasants and farmers, such towns – especially those, like Irvine, with a port – were growing into mercantile centres, full of trade in foreign goods, full of the sound of organized industry replacing the eident toil of the family cottage. Roads needed improving, old wooden houses were torn down and replaced with brick garrets. The local gentry, in the form of the Earl of Eglinton – whose estate rolled away from the north of Irvine, banking Kilwinning – invested the family money in sunken coal pits and ironworks, and the face of the area was altered for good. The vagrancy and beggary that were to disappear early in the twentieth century, then reappear towards the end of it, were rife in the midst of this age. Irvine Council had to set aside money for a public kitchen – there was a notorious meal mob in 1777 – and this kitchen, though redundant at the onset of the welfare state, was again instituted, this time by volunteers, in the Irvine of 1994.

The town's harbour, in the earlier century as now, was forever silting up. But it was dredged, and before the first deepening of the Clyde, boats from America and the West Indies would dock at Irvine, and their cargo would be taken to Glasgow by cart. So, in a handful of years, this rather backward locality became full of bustle and trade; success showed itself in the building of town houses, the design of elaborate churches, and the buying up of surrounding land for redevelopment. But it

75

was also a time of religious zealotry, a time when the poor got poorer as the rich did well, a time of disease and public disorder. It was the age that ripened inequality, but also the one that made grand advancements in civic development. The schools at Irvine, especially the Royal Academy, were thought to be among the best in the country, and education – including that offered at a nautical school run by Robert Burns's friend David Sillar – was counted high. There was suddenly a bookshop, Templeton's in the High Street, and newspapers from London, along with the hot political and literary journals of the day. In a flash, Irvine became a town that was part of the world, and a place connected to the ideas that were turning that world upside-down.

This is the Irvine of the novelist John Galt, who was born at a house in the High Street in 1779. He was the son of a sea captain, and he didn't keep well, but as a child he scurried around this changing locality, chasing the world that was going, and greeting the new one coming in. His novels, written many years later but set in this fictional Irvine (called Irwin or Gudetown) map out, in miniature, with personal coloration, in Flemish detail, this little Scottish town in the grip of monumental change. If he has themes, they are to do with extinction and renewal, but mostly he has characters, kenspeckled local worthies who speak in their own way. Provosts and reverends, beadles and seamstresses, shopkeepers and magistrates and drunken town-drummers.

Galt's Jeanie Tirlet and Marion Sapples, the washerwomen, did the big washing on the low green, on an expanse of grass by the river where we would play in our own time. Down the women would march, 'with a pickle tea and sugar tied in the corners of a napkin, and two measured glasses of whisky in an old doctor's bottle'. The much-married Revd Micah Bal-whidder, hero of *Annals of the Parish*, grows annoyed at the brutal games of the children in the High Street, once the site of light-hearted daffing on clear days. Galt is writing of a fictional location – not fiction at all – which is precisely the area we would beat up and daff on ourselves, in the summer months of our own youth. Galt didn't like the word novel; he thought, in these little master-pieces of town life and character, that he was writing 'theoretical histories'.

The books are full of places (and types) still very much there in the town, and – as if to stress the way such books can alter our sense of place – many of the closes and streets around the town now are named after Galt's supposedly fictional charac-ters. The tall, beady-eyed scribe left Irvine as a boy, lost a fortune in prospecting schemes in Canada and elsewhere, and returned to London, to a sad stint as editor of the *Courier*, to a spell in gaol, to a falling out with Blackwood, his bullying but far-sighted publisher, and to the admiration of Coleridge and Carlyle. He would finish up in Greenock, dying in his sister's small house, but he would continue to think of the strangely penetrating time and place that occasioned his *Tales of the West*. Irvine, like everywhere else by the time of his death, was travelling under steam. Generations were coming who would only know the old town – buried beneath their glittering new one – from the magic of Galt's little histories, his freehand illustrations, his sinister portraits. 'Memory,' he wrote, 'occasionally carries me back to transactions that must have happened when I was very young.' Those occasions were ripe: Galt's memory carries forward, helping many who came after to live in such towns properly, that is to say imaginatively, as well as in body.

The Irvine of Galt's youth was a place full of piety and argument. He gives many clues to the origins of such pressures, and aided my attempts to look at those in the Ayrshire of my own time. The Church of Scotland ruled – the kirk was fitted to take eighteen hundred people, and it did so every Sunday – but splinter groups and secessionists abounded. As a boy, Galt was often to be seen among the tombstones in the graveyard by the kirk. He loved churches, and found in them little 'clues of experience, and shapings of matter'. The Trinity Church, a Venetian Gothic affair planted less than two minutes from the old kirk, is the one with the tall steeple I remember seeing from the high flats on the hairdressing day, throwing its long shadow on those workers making way for the new shopping mall across the river in 1974. On the river's opposite bank, the Fullarton Church sat quiet, about to be shrouded by the mall's giant plastic skin. For hundreds of years there was a rumour, now more than a rumour, that a Carmelite convent was buried underneath, and that stones peeping out of the river – stones still called the Friar's Caulfield – were the remnants of an older order. Galt's first memory was to do with the religious sect of Mrs Buchan – a local cult of spiritualists who broke from the Kirk and proclaimed knowledge of the New Jerusalem. They were hounded from the town, and a great procession followed them, howling and merry-making, and jostling the Buchanites on their way. The infant Galt followed the procession, losing himself, and stocking up on every look.

John Knox described Ayrshire as 'a Receptacle of God's Saints'. The Roman Catholics failed to survive the Reformation in this area – ruined abbeys and buried monasteries still peep through the new constructions – and the Catholics have returned only since the nineteenth century. There was, in Galt's

Irvine, a preserved sense that a Catholic individual was a sort of witch. Plenty of witches were burned at the market cross in previous generations. One, Margaret Barclay, was strangled and burnt at the stake for cursing a local ship, the *Gift of God*, which later foundered off the coast of Cornwall. And the skeleton of the heretic Jean Swan, who murdered her baby in 1760, stood in the laboratory of Irvine Royal Academy for over a hundred years. When the town ran out of witches and child-murderers to torch, there was always – lingering in the back of the mind – the thought of Catholics. Galt's Revd Balwhidder sums up the local antagonism: 'Fortunately, for my peace of mind, there proved to be but five Roman Catholics [. . .] and Father O'Grady, not being able to make a living there, packed up his Virgin Maries, saints, and painted Agnuses in a portmanteau, and went off in the Ayr flier one morning for Glasgow, where I hear he has since met with all the encouragement that might be expected from the ignorant and idolatrous inhabitants of that great city.'

The first actual Catholic priest in Ayrshire came in 1822, like most of us, from Ireland (though not, like many of us later idolaters, via Glasgow). He opened a mission in Ayr and travelled to town and village on horseback. Father William Fitzgerald came to Irvine in 1862, and set up the 'lum kirk', a three-chimneyed chapel much resented by the local community. Two years later, there was already a local group of Orangemen; the area was to remain fiercely Protestant. The gains of the Reformation were still spitefully contested, and just as spitefully refused, in an Ayrshire stretching into the future. The locals, as much as the in-comers, wanted to be as much themselves as they'd always been. The west coast of Scotland was never an easy place to be yourself anyway, but as the years passed, and the modern topsoil spread over everything else, people in the area continued to remember who the traditional enemy was. As we know, there's sometimes too much pleasure, and too much social cohesion, involved in an ongoing mutual hatred for it to be surrendered just like that. In the absence of much else, of course, prejudice is a form of tradition.

MY FIRST DAY at St Winnin's RC I recall in slow motion, coloured yellow and brown. It was, and is, more frightening than romantic, and I cried all the way to the school gate. Things had begun to take off with my visit to the high flats at Irvine. I suddenly knew more about the world, and saw our black and white housing estate as a sort of adventure park that opened onto lots of differently coloured and gradually aged surroundings. To get to the school, you had to walk about a mile, through open fields full of cement-mixers and dumpers. Squads of men were laying foundations, putting up walls and prefab units, building Pennyburn's phase two. Starting school was a fantastic ritual: the gear was put on you, your hair was wetted and slicked, and you were stood in the square while neighbours gathered around to point and pinch and stuff coins into the pockets of your new blazer. The blazer, I remember, felt heavy. It had a green and gold badge stitched onto the top pocket, the tie was already knotted, put over your head in one go, and held in place with an elastic loop. The trousers were charcoal and long, and the shoes squeaky. You knew it was the start of something big.

I stood in line at the doors opening onto the playground, turning round every other second, crying, and watching the faces of the mothers biting their nails and waving through the bars of the gate. We were led inside. I'd never smelt a room like it before. The classroom was high windowed and cold, and it had the roving odour of pee and Plasticine. The teacher seemed old, though she was probably only forty-something, and she smelt like a maternity nurse. In other words, she smelt of sick. She warned those of us still sniffling that we'd better stop it right away, and she gave each child a paper doily and felt-tips and told us to colour it in. That was that, and the rest of those first days in Primary One were taken up with colouring-in duty, or standing at a plastic sandpit, or sploshing paint onto slabs of grey card. It became fun, and the room grew familiar. Mrs Nugent's face was all rubbery, and I can very clearly remember it mouthing the word 'apple' over and over. 'Ap-ple.' There were lines around her mouth, they'd stretch and then her lips would bash together every time. 'Ap-ple.' We all said it, and the noise in the room sounded big and crunchy. After saying it for ages, Mrs Nugent shushed us, and pinned a large 'A' above the blackboard. We were learning to read.

Before long, there was a line of letters, the alphabet, right across the blackboard wall, and she handed out books. I feel funny describing it – books would become the most important thing of all. But it didn't feel like it on the day; the one she gave me felt slimy and was hard to understand. It only had a few words on each page, and a very big picture. Mrs Nugent showed all her teeth, and read out the title. '*Dick, Dora, Nip and Fluff.*' The sandpit and the paints were never to be so interesting again. Like the afternoon cartoons and the hairdressing journeys with my mum that were now part of something called the past, these books would suggest a world fuller than suspected. I really admired Dick and Dora, and the way they went to the park and brushed their teeth and lived in a square house out on its own. They gave an idea of a universal community of children; all the same, all here to stay, and to stay for ever the same. There was no darkness and doubt in the world of Dick and Dora, no effort involved in keeping clean, no hurt, no worry or bad weather. The rain was a problem to be solved, usually with an umbrella, and it was generally an excuse for cheerfulness and good character. Dick and Dora knew much more about how to be simple and good in the world than anyone I'd met; they knew everything, and I supposed that was why they were in a book. I already knew, just in the way that you do, that the world – or the world of Pennyburn, at least – wasn't entirely like that. With these little paperbacks, a private world was opening up too, and for years it would play on its own, increasingly removed from the world outside. There would always be Dick and Dora, then Joby, and Black Beauty, and my pal Spadger, to fill the head full of good thoughts, or just thoughts. The noble acts and pure hearts of people in books would be lapped up and loved, but never lived up to. In time we'd read of them, sigh, and go outside, to a place where other influences, other instincts – other knowledge – drove us into fits of childish cruelty and badness never noted in our beloved tomes.

We started praying to Mary at about the same time as we began to read. She wore a blue dress and had roses for shoes. In pictures, she always had her hands up, or clapped together, and she'd be floating in the air. It isn't just any old blue, that sky, it's the sort of blue that stands for goodness and purity and not for Rangers. That is what we'd hear, although not from everybody. Our Lady would do good things for us, if we sent her our prayers and good wishes. We could learn the rosary, and say it for her. She was God's mother and if there was anything we wanted and he was too busy to hear us, we could tell Mary and she'd tell Jesus – who was God's son but was God as well. It wasn't long till our First Holy Communions, then we'd know all about it. Those who taught religion at that school were pretty strict, very bitter, and they always encouraged us to feel that we were very privileged not to be Protestants. We were chosen, and we had the most beautiful churches of all, the most wonderful statues and crosses that we could kneel in front of. We thought we were great, and the classroom was soon full of our drawings of pregnant Mary and sheepish Joseph, trudging, with their grids of teeth, after the brilliant star.

Father MacLaughlin had thick glasses and a weird voice. He was from Ireland and was always yawning and telling us about the Bad Fire. He used the word evil, and talked about grace and sacraments and confession. Yes indeed, the Bad Fire was there for people who couldn't be good, you'd die unloved and unblessed and go to the Bad Fire if you didn't *a*. be good, *b*. not tell lies, *c*. pray, *d*. eat fish on a Friday, *e*. love your mummy and daddy and do what they told you, *f*. go to chapel, *g*. cross yourself morning and night, and bless the Pope, *h*. do something for Lent, *i*. be nice to nuns and not cheek back the priests, *j*. adore the saints, *k*. remember not to drink Holy Water, *l*. make your First Holy Communion in a white dress (girls) or red sash (boys), *m*. get confirmed when you were in primary six, *n*. marry a Catholic, *o*. marry in the chapel, *p*. confess everything, *q*. go to devotions once in a while, *r*. get a priest quickly when you think you are going to die, *s*. ignore the Orange Walk – stay in on the Twelfth, or go to the pictures, *t*. do your full penance after confession; no hurrying it up, *u*. help with church cleaning sometimes, and think about joining the Legion of

Mary, *v.* stop touching yourself, *w.* stop doing the Ouija board, and doubting the Immaculate Conception, *x.* lay off the drink, and never smoke fags or start fires, *y.* stop chapping the chapel-house door and running away, and *z.* resist having abortions, or sexual intercourse outside of marriage, or using contraception, or getting divorced without the Pope's say-so. This was Father MacLaughlin's creed: he wanted us all 'to meet one day in heaven' and these were the conditions. We were all pretty fascinated, and wondered what he was talking about, but we promised ourselves never to do it again, and made the sign of the cross. Father MacLaughlin spoke like God, but he didn't look like Him. His eyebrows gathered in the middle of his head, and he made me sure that whatever it was, I was never going to do it ever ever again.

I knew that people could die. I remembered the budgie being called dead, and then, of course, there was the priest before MacLaughlin, Father Burke, who Michael had seen green and dead in his coffin. These stuck in my mind, and I knew that death was terrible, especially if it meant the Bad Fire. But I thought that only animals and old people could die or go away; children were invincible and always around. We could do anything to each other, so long as it wasn't too sore, and nothing would happen. Mrs Wallace was my second teacher, and she taught me how to write things down. She was gruff and kind, with curly red hair. She obviously liked some kids more than others. She would get me to do favours for her, running around and taking messages. She liked me to read for the class, but would often stop me, slap my hand, and say 'off by heart, you're reading it off by heart'. I had no idea what she meant by that, but obviously, now that I think of it, I must have rehearsed the readings and made some of it up as I went along. In 1975, we made our First Holy Communions, and I had my photos taken on top of a furry rug in Saltcoats. We never picked the photos up, but I have the certificate somewhere. We had cakes and a disco round the back of St Winnin's Chapel, in the hall, right after the Mass, and all I kept thinking was Jesus, that bread's chewy – it's the body of Christ.

By that time, they'd built a new Catholic primary for kids from the scheme, and it sat right in the corner of Pennyburn. It was called St Luke's, and we transferred there as the first class. We'd only been there a few weeks when Mrs Wallace died. I heard the new teacher say 'cancer' and I later looked it up. Mrs Wallace was dead of cancer. A group of us from St Luke's went to the funeral Mass, and we all sat singing hymns with the coffin there. I was very confused, but Father MacLaughlin explained it all, and said she was certainly in a better place. Behind the priest, mounted on the wall in front of the altar, was the biggest statue I'd ever seen. It was truly colossal, this thing, at least thirty feet from top to bottom. It was a wooden carving of Jesus on the cross, and it was mesmerizing. His hands were pinned to the wood with giant bolts, blood ran down in thick lines. His feet rested on a wee platform, but were hammered in, with more blood showing. All the limbs looked thin and a bit blue and crooked. Thorns were twined round his head, crushed down, and more blood ran down his forehead. He'd a cloth round his bum, and his eyes were looking up. It looked so sore, and I had loads of questions. But I didn't say anything; I just filed up with everyone else in my row for chewy bread. When I came back, they were singing a new song, and someone had already pulled down the kneeling cushion for us to say our prayers on.

MY MUM WAS still cleaning at the Protestant primary, and

sometimes I'd go down there after school to watch her mop, and to read the books while she Hoovered. After she had done the carpets, I'd often go around her classrooms, or those of the other women, taking the chairs down from the tables and putting everything back into place. I'd wander through the corridors while they were having their tea, making sure not to step on any wet tiles as I went. The boss in this situation was always the janitor, and there was one in particular that I liked from this time. He was called Jimmy. He was one of those hardmen, always marching around chewing gum and swinging a hideous, glittering bunch of keys. Jimmy would let me into the music room to bang on the piano and play the tambourine. He was good that way, and sometimes he'd open up the tuck shop and give me something from it. He had tattoos all the way up his arms, they were all in blue and were more like words than pictures. But I think there was a flag. He'd be sweeping with a brush, and I'd be dancing on the stage, wrapping myself up in the velvety curtain. There was also a model in the school that I became fascinated with; it was of the whole housing scheme, and was made of polystyrene and bits of sponge. All the houses, like the one we stayed in, were built on it, and all the squares in the grid were built in carefully. Bits of sponge painted green were placed to represent patches of grass and flower-bed. Below the railway line on the model were rows of houses which didn't exist then. They exist now, but at that time they were still being planned and built. This model showed how the scheme would be ten years hence, and it had me gripped. It looked like a space-village, like something that had never been thought of before.

Jimmy was arrested one day and taken away by the police. He was a member of the UDA, and he'd been smuggling arms out of Scotland for years. Everyone was shocked; he got four-teen years. They were all shaking their heads about it, and looking at his photo in the *Daily Record*. Although many of the 'overspillers', the ones from Glasgow, had come looking for a new way of life, a new start, it turned out not to be that straightforward. The new town had some jobs then, and had much to offer, but it wasn't a place without division and bigotry. A lot of the old city ways were brought down, and set up in the new housing schemes much as before. The place was transformed by all this. It was, although we didn't realize it until later, a place with much tradition of its own, measures of it good and bad just like anywhere else. But the great influx of people from outside made a big difference; although it had tons of factories, the place had never entirely lost its rural feel. But the new housing schemes, in the sixties way, had nothing to do with that. The new concrete world, the landscaping, was grafted onto the fields, roads were driven through, and a certain template for living, different from the old local ways of doing it, was laid down.

This is how it seems to me now. There was no such thinking about it at the time, of course; nobody was thinking that way, we were either too young or too busy just living, too taken up with our new lives to think about what all this newness actually meant. The past, our past, was obliterated, though I can't say what made us so sure, apart from the prevailing wish among our kind to have a better life, at all costs. We weren't that disappointed, and our new schemes were built to correspond to our wishes, and to nothing else round about or beyond it. As I scan these memories I keep running into the thud of significance, that came, in these circumstances, from the knowl-edge that violence and bad ways weren't left behind at all. They were part of the mythology of a distant city, yes, but things began to happen which seemed to show that the old habits, the darker tints, were actually there with us, growing in the new world.

The arrest of Jimmy Hamilton strikes me like that; it seemed like a situation from another place and another time, and not the sort of thing that was expected of the new town at all. Reading this, you might find what I say a bit surprising. I mean, you might think it perfectly understandable that Glasgow and the new town should be alike; after all, they are very close and perhaps only locals would see such a gulf between these two obviously similar places? That is a point, and one that I hope is absorbed into this account of what seemed to happen during those years. Part of what our experience was, indeed, has to do with a sort of disaffection at the realization that these two kinds of community were actually the same. We didn't expect that, and there can be no underestimating just how much hope and high expectation was invested in what must seem such an ordinary local move. It didn't seem like that to our parents. It didn't seem at all ordinary. It seemed, to parents like mine, like a gigantic step into the unknown, away from all their familiar haunts, free of all that was troubling and dark. It was a step towards some sort of light, and such moves, even in small countries, can seem monumental.

Local gangs started to form and do battle. In 1975, in the centre of Irvine, the police baton-charged a notorious group called Apache, whose use of open blades was a terrible reminder to some, and a terrible innovation to others. In Pennyburn, the local gang was called Priesty – after the area of Priesthill, in Glasgow – and you'd see the initials of the gang (YTP: Young Tiny Priesty) scratched into every surface imaginable. The hard-nuts who weren't part of the overspill – people actually born in the local area – formed gangs to battle with the in-comers. The mock-seriousness of the names still makes me laugh. One was called The Vambo, another was The Cumbie. The Priesty were, by turns, timid and ferocious; they egged each other on, and fights grew increasingly bloody. My brother Michael worked in the chippy, and the gang, including some of his mates, would hang around outside, planning retributions and petty thefts as if secluded in a war bunker.

You'd often see them, middle-shedded teenagers in the seventies, flares and platforms intact, suit collars wide and fronts covered in buttons, twirling sticks round their backs outside the chip shop, planning a game or a battle charge. I was up at my bedroom window one evening, fiddling with a plastic typewriter, when I saw a commotion in the car park at the top of the square. Boys were running and scattering, and there was shouting going on. I saw a boy with red hair who lived in the next square to us, one of a big family, charging after someone and wielding something that looked like an axe. There was fear and madness in his face, and he was chasing, or being chased. As I lay down on my bed I heard something downstairs: it was nothing, one of my brothers had slipped in the door and was walking to the press to put away his coat.

I WAS EIGHT in 1976, and I didn't feel much like a baby or a toddler. I could walk around, and read; I could tell you what was going on in the squares. I was suddenly less shy, and my life became full of action at school and danger abroad. The breathing things that really dominate housing schemes, and back-courts and residential streets, aren't adults – forever on their way to cars or other buildings – but children and dogs. There were dogs everywhere; kids rolled with all sorts of mutleys in the dirt, and drove scampering packs, like teams of huskies, down the lanes and through the tunnels with sticks. The life of the classroom, and the drone of Mother's Hoover, had nothing in the way of excitement when compared with the unsupervised life outside. We really came into our own out there, and we found a way to adopt characteristics that adults would have thought out of character; from each other we learnt new ways; we achieved strength in numbers; nothing was any danger.

In my memory, 1976 was the year of a new sort of independence, hitherto only enjoyed in snatches, foolish moments when parents' backs were turned. We displayed a new sort of guile. Or, more accurately, we guilefully failed to show the measures of new guile we'd somehow acquired. I'd long since seen the old picture of my granda Michael by then, and I wondered what sort of person lived in Glasgow. I mean, I knew that we used to live there, and I knew what we were like, but the city – in our childish talk – held a certain mystery and fascination that I think was to do with what we'd heard older boys say about it. It was hard. You'd hear them talk of how rough it was, how tough they were for coming down from there so recently. Some of them spoke out of the side of their mouths in the Cagney fashion, and would tell of how certain kinds of crap, local crap, the Ayrshire dung, as it were, would never have been tolerated by this or that heroic Glasgow mob.

We didn't understand how things worked, and we took things too far. Our most serious purpose was the search for fun, and this became an increasingly dangerous business, and often a notably violent one. In that year, I think we found out how bad we could be. Around that time, I was in the habit of walking to school in the company of a blonde girl from the other side of the square. I'll call her Katie. We were in the same class, and she was sort of my girlfriend. We liked to play at offices on her doorstep, with loads of pads and typewriters, but we'd often get fed up with that and imagine ourselves into something else. We got to taking a little boy to school in the morning, little David, and we were fond of taunting him along the way. The workies on the building sites would give us lemonade bottles to cash in for sweets, and we'd scoff the sweets, and leave David out. We started to play at being his mummy and daddy, and hitting him for being bad. It was just a few slaps at first, but it got worse. There were freshly planted trees around the place, tied to stalks with rubber belts. We started taking them off on the journey, and whipping David with them. Eventually, one morning, very late for assembly, we were caught on a railway bridge near the school, practically skinning the boy's legs. He was screaming and we were laughing and hitting like crazy. The teachers caught us and our parents battered us in return, but it was nowhere near the end of it.

There was another David, a very young boy who lived at number three. He lived there alone with his mum and sometimes she'd let us take him outside, to sort of babysit. We were playing in the field one day, under the television mast, and we found a swamp which was quite deep in the middle. We were throwing boulders in, and trying the depth out with washing poles, until we got bored. There were four boys there, four plus the toddler David, who couldn't speak. We got him to sit down in the marsh, and started trying to press him in deeper with the poles. He was crying, and soaking, and we would cuddle him better then put him back in. We didn't know what we were doing, I think, but we knew that it was dangerous and it was giving a dangerous thrill. Usually, as in this case, sense at last got the better of us, and we lifted him out and took him crying to his mother. We pretended he'd fallen in and that we'd saved him. We didn't regret it, and we didn't celebrate it. It was just something that had happened. As time went on, we knew quite a lot about situations of that kind, and we knew that parents didn't see much of it. Only now and then would things go too far, and then we'd all be in for it.

We'd go camping on the school playing-fields at night, and never go to sleep. A game of hide and seek with torches would sometimes turn into a game of hunting down small animals or cats to worry or kill. We got into petty vandalism on these trips, and loved to wreck gardens, break countless milk bottles and panes of glass. There was a place called Todhill Farm on the outskirts of our estate. It was a training farm for young men with Down's syndrome, and it sat just under the dual carriageway that was being built in 1976. We'd go down there with our torches – the Toadies, we'd whisper, the Toadies are loonies – and wreck their work. They had fields of carrots and strawberries which they tended every day, and there we'd be, leaping and tearing in the dark, and carrying off bags of fat strawberries in plastic bags brought specially for the purpose. Kids like us gave those Down's boys a terrible time. Even in broad daylight, we'd terrorize them, and chase them over the fields on our Grifters or Choppers or whatever those chunky bikes were called. It became difficult to see the difference between fun and brutality, between bad-boyish misdemeanours and hellish bad-bastardness. Now and again, when you'd a certain group of marauding kids bouncing malevolent sparks off each other, you would think you were untouchable. There's no pride in it, but that's the way it was.

One or two of the boys assiduously built bridges between this sort of behaviour and the ways of adult crime, but the great majority did no such thing. They were never perceived to be problem kids, just kids who sometimes went too far with things. They grew up and mostly forgot this aspect of what it was like being a child, and they didn't take it along with them. That was the norm. I mean, however outrageous this sort of thing now seems in the telling, at the time it didn't seem horrific, it just seemed daft. My little group were actually thought to be quite good natured; their brutalities were secret ones, their adventures were mostly unthought about. All the parents I knew would give their kids a proper doing if they found them out. I remember my brother Charlie and I went off for the day with a team of boys from Garallan Square – one of the squares in the scheme thought to be especially rough. It was a cool day, and we were all skidding around in T-shirts. One kind of adventure would blend into another, and we ended the day by breaking into Palmer's Yard, the site of a local construction firm. We broke every window in the place, emptied jars of coffee all over the offices, the older ones drove dumpers through doors, broke up the floor with hydraulic drills, and shattered the windscreens of lorries. A young classmate of mine, Sharon Mills, was watching all this from an upstairs window in her house nearby, and her mother phoned for the police. My da belted us for that, and then, unaccountably, went off to the sink to throw up.

When I was trying to make sense of a very brutal child murder a few years ago, a murder committed by two ten-year-old boys in Liverpool, I started to recall this period in my own life. It's perfectly natural, though not always right, that people should want to separate themselves from criminal acts they feel they could never commit themselves. But it seemed to me there was something unhelpful about the way that case was discussed. It wasn't the sort of case that anybody was going to understand, but it was one in which the lives of the boys, the lives of such children in general, could bear a little thinking about. Instead the two Scouse boys were called devils, treated as complete anomalies, and they were hounded outside the court by adults sick with the desire for retribution. They were given an adult trial and had their identities exposed in the papers. It seemed to me very strange. They were children, and in some ways they were very typical little boys. Something had gone very badly wrong, obviously. I can't say I identified with them. All I can say is there were certain things about them which were recognizable, things about their lives, their ways of walking and inclining their heads towards each other. Their stance ignited memories that I'd never had reason to think much about, and my editor suggested I write them down.

I realized something. When I thought about my childhood, one of the things I thought of was the measure of childish violence in it, and I'd always wanted to pick it out from the map of my early days. To know more about it, I reckoned, was to know more about the little difficulties of the past, not only my past but the past of my family, and the past of those places where my family had settled. It was a way of staring it straight in the face. The dark tints we might have left behind in the city were with us all right in our new abode, they were more than with us, they were in us. At least, that was one way of thinking about it. My way. And I followed the pattern, absorbing more about my places and times than I'd been able to reach before. The memory of sporadic wickedness opened the way to the larger account. It allowed me to find what was in fact a theme of my growing up. That theme was not violence itself, but the threat of violence returned. It was the threat of something taking me away, stopping my presence, making me disappear. I think I had an irrational fear of disappearance throughout my first days. The childish violence of 1976, and before, and after, would stay linked in my mind to the threat of disappearance. You might wonder why the threat of violence returned would take the form of bodily disappearance, and I'll tell you now. In that year, in the midst of our secret knowledge of all that we were capable of, a child went missing in our area, and then someone else did, and I heard of more people, and this was always something I sought to understand. It was a double-edged worry: it was, we knew, the sort of thing that children could conceivably cause to happen to other children; it was also, I imagined, the sort of thing that could happen to children who knew more than they ought to about such things. People could disappear. My grandfather had disappeared, but that was war. Sandy Davidson was only three.

They thought he might have been buried under one of the new houses, or accidentally covered over with sand, or else abducted. We knew what it was like on the building sites, we played in them all the time. We would join in the searches for Sandy, combing fields and sites around our bit. I wondered about him all the time. Sandy. What could've happened to him? I thought I knew something. I knew something about children's fearsome cruelty, and their passion for misadventure, and I found it not unthinkable that he might have been covered by children little older than himself, at play in a makeshift sandpit. I kept having nightmares about numbers – numbers clicking up and up and out of control. I'd wake up hot and shaking in the dark, and would count back in tens or hundreds until I got to zero, then everything was OK. I'd count in my head, until the number was nothing. I'd sit up in my bunk, and calm down, and try to think clearly. But what, I'd think . . . what if someone has taken Sandy away in a van?

CHRISTMAS, 1994. I wanted to get the train across the New Town – only one stop, Kilwinning to Irvine – and I left my mother's house in plenty of time. I followed a pattern of very familiar paths, cutting through the estate and leading to the station. It occurred to me that the paths were made in a funny way. The tiny and glittery white stones that clothed the houses were sprinkled in with the path's Tarmac as well. It was a bit frosty this day, and the bits in the path glittered even more than usual. I could remember, years ago, trying to dig those stones out with a metal spoon on days when the tar was gooey with the sun. I liked the thought, and I fancied I could see – though I couldn't – little spaces in the ground where kids had been digging through the tar more recently. On my way to the railway station, I also passed a bit of waste ground that caused me to smirk. It was the site of a famous local hotel called the Winton Arms. It had been bought out a few years ago, painted with gloss, and renamed the Railway Inn, but to everybody around here it was still the Winton. It was just an empty space now, but it had once been one of the most notorious and most curious places in the town.

The hotel, run by a woman called Lily with a withered hand, had been famous for not letting Catholics in. Lily was bitter, and was steeped in the area's great enmities. But none was greater to her, as a threat, as something of an outrage too, than the continued presence of Catholics in Kilwinning. I used to go out with a girl who worked for her, not in the hotel but in her outside-catering business. She would tell me about Lily's hilarious doctoring of the Papish victuals – the wedding and funeral baked meats – on the very rare occasions when they catered for a Catholic social event. Into the pot Lily's nerveless paw would go, pink as a pig's trotter, stirring the Irish stew for all her venom and spit was worth. She'd mumble Orange anthems under her breath as she passed round the plates of buttered bread, our Lily, and she was well known for it. I was still laughing to myself about this as I got on the train.

'Don't start me,' said this drunk across the way. Not that I was going to, but his warning was enough of a threat to stop me from ever making eye contact as long as we both shall live. I stared out of the window instead, and watched my mother's house, with all the others, blur past in a loop of black-and-white. You got a good view of the New Town from up there. The ICI works – opened as Nobel's Explosives in 1874 – looked like nothing now; the huge pipes that used to stretch up so frighteningly high were gone, and much of the plant was closed. I remember our classroom windows shaking with the blast when they were testing their dynamite in the seventies; a giant bang, and we'd all be up looking out, wondering how the hell those cooling towers could stand up. There were two of them then, and I was always inventing stories about how the man who painted them had a giant ladder, how he'd been painting the rim once when he fell in and was burned in the fire at the bottom. The Bad Fire. It was all clear sea air around there now, and their absence made you feel that you were in a different place. I'd read in a local newspaper that the Irvine Development Corporation, the ones who founded the New Town in the sixties and have run it since then, were starting to wind up in preparation for their extinction in 1996.

Some things had gone well with the New Town idea; other things had not gone well at all. There were never enough jobs, and targets couldn't be met, and the new firms – non-unionized computer-components firms from Japan and America – employed mainly non-skilled workers for low wages. That was one thing. But a lot of people were happy to say they'd bought their council house during those years; many were just as happy being able to live among the heritage trails, the leisure facilities, and tourist attractions which had made their world a better place. There were more than two ways about it: the old Royal Burgh and the spartan New Town would never entirely settle their differences. As I walked out from the station, and made for the mall across the River Irvine, I caught sight of a new drive-in burger bar, over to the left. It sat on an open space at the edge of the car park. A hundred years before, it was the site of one of the town's most bustling (and decrepit) streets.

The vanished street had been called Fullarton Street, and James Montgomery, one of the most popular of the religious or 'sacred' poets of the nineteenth century, had been born there in 1771. He was the son of a preacher of the Society of United Moravian Brethren and – like John Galt – he left Irvine whilst still a boy. Montgomery would help his generation, and some after that, with their singing to God, and his earthly life was full. He became a famous citizen of Sheffield: he was the editor and proprietor of a weekly magazine called *Iris*, and he was twice imprisoned in York Castle for printing libels. Although he was once considered a rival to William Cowper, he is seldom read these days. But one or two of his hymns are remembered. Not long before walking past the non-place of his birth, I found a humorous poem of his which made me think of Agnes, my mum. It's a bad poem, but it funnily catches my mother's weakness for scolding, and my weakness for tormenting her by acting the know-all. It's called 'To Agnes' and it came into my head as I walked towards the mall:

> Time will not check his eager flight,
> Though gentle Agnes scold,
> For 'tis the sage's dear delight
> To make young ladies old.

> Then listen, Agnes, friendship sings;
> Seize fast his forelock grey,
> And pluck from his careering wings
> A feather every day.

The security cameras take pictures of people doing their ordinary thing. The mall is thronged with them, people loaded down with post-Christmas bags of shopping. Walking down, I looked on a stream of half-familiar faces; and I thought I knew some of those mothers trailing toddlers behind them on lengths of cord. The shops were bright and inviting. I'd worked in several of them as a teenager – selling shoes, stacking shelves – and could see the staff were as harassed and bad tempered as they used to be. I stopped for a second halfway down, and looked through the glass at the river underneath. It was racing through its channel; and the low green on the right bank was still not fully recovered from recent flooding. The mall was full of blowing and whirring convector heat. It was warm and full of tinsel, wrapped against the day outside. But the thing about malls – the good and the bad thing about malls – is that you have to come out the other end some time. It's like coming out of the cinema, or out of an especially sexy dream: you're suddenly there in the world you actually live in, with people you actually know, and it's all a bit actual. I made my way to the police station, which sits round the back of the tollbooth.

Sandy Jardine Davidson, the little blond boy who vanished in 1976, had caused me to be here. He'd caused me to be many places this last while, and I felt like I was trailing him. I was determined to know more about what had happened on that day, 23 April 1976, and I thought there might be other clues, other possibilities, that could explain it all. Looking for Sandy, I had always found more of ourselves, more of our community, but he was still missing, and the facts of his disappearance were slim and unchanging.

It had been a nice morning that day. Sandy and his younger sister Donna were being looked after by their granny, Mary Bunce, who lived at 38 St Kilda Bank, on the Bourtreehill estate. Like many other parts of the town, Bourtreehill was only half-built in that year. Many of the houses were having the final work done to them; and many were still at the foundations stage. But quite a few had families already living in them. Margaret Davidson was twenty-two, her husband Philip was twenty-five and they'd moved to the new estate just six weeks before. They lived just up the road from Margaret's mother, at number 41. They'd gone off to work that morning as usual, leaving the children and the dog, Kissie, in the company of Mrs Bunce.

Sandy was three, and was able to play in the garden and in the area just beyond it, which at that time was just open waste. He was wearing a three-button pullover. It was purple, with a tiny motif on the side saying 'Small Men'. He'd on long mauve-coloured check trousers, and wore blue and white sandshoes with the initials GB printed on them. At 10.25 Sandy came into the house to tell his granny that Kissie had run off. 'Don't chase it,' she said. Sandy went back out. A few minutes later Donna came into the room and told her that Sandy had gone to the water. Mr and Mrs Bunce went outside, and started scouring the stretch of ground between the house and the River Annick, which bordered the bottom of the estate. They couldn't find him, and in a rising panic, they rushed here and there, expecting to find him any second. Kissie was sitting on the doorstep. By eleven o'clock, they were frantic, and they phoned Irvine police station. The report was taken by Inspector Reid and Sergeant Ross. They took a description, and initiated a search of the area.

There was heavy earth-moving equipment in Bourtreehill that morning. There were workmen all over the place; culverts were being dug; pipes laid. This worried the police, and when the search for Sandy had got nowhere by the late afternoon, they set up a caravan on the site and called in more personnel. They brought in sniffer dogs and divers too. The Annick was sectioned off, and combed by frogmen repeatedly. Massive ground searches were organized, which soon involved dozens of people in the area. They sifted through the piles of sand and debris which had been moved that morning, but found nothing. Superintendent Frank James led the operation, and it was one that grew bigger by the hour. One of the empty houses in the street, just two hundred yards from Sandy's home, was set up as the police headquarters, and volunteers supplied tea and things from there, to both the police and the civilians involved in the searches. By late in the evening, with everything dark, the operation had to be postponed till the following day.

Mrs Bunce had collapsed in the afternoon and was being attended by a doctor. Margaret Davidson was experiencing a sort of panic and fear which can't be described. Mr Davidson was out with the search, and couldn't believe the worst. They thought he might have been taken away in a van. 'A year ago Sandy climbed into a van and he was discovered in Lanarkshire,' said Philip Davidson. 'Instinct tells the whole family that Sandy is alive. He has been taken by someone in a car. We can only hope and pray for Sandy, but one thing is sure, the whole family will throw a huge party when he returns home.'

Derelict brickworks just over the road in the town of Dreghorn were being combed by experts, led by Alistair Findlay, a twenty-nine-year-old potholer from Glasgow. He spoke of dozens of tunnels and kilns with passageways leading underground. 'In many of them,' he said, 'we had to crawl among the rubble on our hands and knees in the dark.' In an effort to establish what had happened to Sandy, every nook and cranny of the area was being gone through, every open space, every stretch of water, every house, had to be eliminated. Posters were put up on bus shelters and in shop windows, and printed in the local papers. They had a picture of Sandy looking blond and round faced, it was grainy, and underneath it said: 'Has Anybody Seen Sandy?'

WILLIAM MCARTHUR SHOOK my hand firmly, and took me along corridors smelling sometimes of floor-cleaner and sometimes of coffee to a small interview room at the back of Irvine station. He seemed a wee bit nervous, as if very unused to this sort of thing, and not entirely sure of himself, or me. He spoke carefully. An accent of the Ayrshire sort – one so full of tucks, dead ends, swallowed syllables, and clipped corners – cannot be easily finessed. But on the telephone, or speaking to people you don't know, you will often find a sort of politeness laying itself over the rails of your accent, as if this was the professional thing to do. I realized, as I sat across from Detective Constable McArthur in this very formal manner, that we were speaking to each other not in a way that was officious, or put on, but in a way that was quite careful. We wanted to acknowledge the gravity of our discussion, and this meant not sounding like you were in the King's Arms across the road.

Mr McArthur was among the police officers brought into the Sandy Davidson inquiry from other towns in the area. He was involved in the endless door-to-door enquiries, and the collation of information on a card index. The computer method used nowadays, called HOMES (Home Office Major Enquiries System), didn't exist then, and everything had to be taken down and cross-referenced manually. 'Nowadays,' said Mr McArthur, 'you just need to put part of a name into the computer terminal, say, DAV, and the Davidsons, all the Davidsons, every Davidson, comes up.' Much had changed, he indicated, but much had stayed the same. The search for Sandy involved a lot of people searching the area for traces, for anything at all that might give a clue, but they were unable to continue searching indefinitely. They had to give up some time. 'When,' I asked, 'when would you decide that an inquiry had come to its end?'

'Well, you explore every sort of avenue and exhaust every possible line of enquiry,' he said. 'The Sandy Davidson inquiry went on not just for months, it went on for years. After the main incident room was shut down, things still came in . . . spiritualists and mediums would come, and you'd have to weigh these things up.' He looked down at the notes: 'But you always get these things.'

'Yes,' I said, 'there's often been a lot of publicity about

Scottish cases where mediums were involved.' I thought about this, about the effort to locate missing killers or the bodies of possible murder victims. 'I mean, they brought them in on the Bible John case.'

'I worked on the Bible John inquiry as well,' said Mr McArthur. 'A lot of the inquiry came down here, to interview people in Ayrshire. And it was tricky, you know; a lot of guys didn't want their wives to know they'd been to the dancehall.' We laughed, and I said that I'd heard that too.

The Sandy Davidson inquiry was one in which there were very few clues; there was little to work on. Someone thought they'd heard a child's scream at the brickworks; someone thought they saw a man with a sky-blue car – a man about forty or so years old, about 5'8" with fair hair – driving off with a little boy at 10.55 on the Friday morning Sandy disappeared. Police helicopters flew over the housing scheme, but found nothing. As the weeks passed, those involved had different theories. Some felt he had fallen asleep and been covered; some felt he had gone into the water and had likely been carried away; others felt he was certainly abducted, probably by someone with a car, possibly by someone living nearby; and still others felt he might have gone into the foundations of a house, and suffered some sort of accident there.

It became one of the most seriously troubling episodes of that decade, at least that's how it felt to many living in the New Town. They couldn't get over it. Mr and Mrs Davidson left the scheme soon after, and went to live in Saltcoats. Two years after it, Margaret Davidson was still pleading for news of her son. 'It's been two years of agony for my husband Philip and myself,' she said. 'I still believe he is alive because if he was dead the police would have found something.'

Mr McArthur stared into his coffee. I told him I'd been thinking the worst. 'If someone had a mind to do it,' I said, 'how easy would it be to dispose of a body in an area like this?'

'There's a lot of missing persons throughout the country,' he said. 'I mean, that Frederick West inquiry, in Gloucester, is an example of how bodies can be disposed of. With West, the bodies were often people who were missing who'd never been reported missing. Daughter murdered, first wife murdered; and not on police files as missing persons. These things happen.' Constable McArthur seemed to relax, and take his coffee less studiously, when I asked him about his own life. He came from one of the smaller Ayrshire mining communities, and worked in the pits for ten years after leaving school. 'My father had been in the Burma campaign,' he said, 'and he didn't want us to ever experience anything like that. And one of the exempted occupations was coal-mining, and that was one of the reasons I went into it. It wasn't really by choice.'

'What was the life like?'

'You could make good money at it,' he said, 'I left the mines to join the police force and took a drop. I started here at Irvine, then went up to Prestwick and then to Ayr in 1968.' He told me about changes in the way local forces are organized, changes in responsibilities, in the volume of crime. 'It's the same every-where in the country,' he said.

We looked again at some of the details of Sandy Davidson's disappearance, and I asked him if the case still comes into his mind, if it still niggles at him.

'Some cases,' he said, 'cause you to realize, after a time, that they'll never be solved. They'll probably remain a mystery.'

I caught a blue bus outside, and sat on the top deck, watching the new town spool past. The woman who came up for my fare was one of those who's been taking fares on the A1 buses, on this route, since I was a child. I'm sure she almost pulled my ear off once, when she found me and my pals crouching behind seats up the back, trying to dodge the fare. She smiled down at me; she was all lacquered and lipsticked, just as I remember her.

THE SUMMER OF 1976 was one of the hottest on record. All of the kids were running about with trunks on (the girls wore tiny swimsuits, with sewn-on skirts) and we were always looking for water to dive into. The lump of grass in the middle of our square became the site of many games, and many troubles. We'd fill up empty Fairy Liquid bottles with water and scoosh each other with them during games of tig or sodjers. We invented a game called Whaddyawant?: someone would stand at the bottom of the hill and ask you that, and you'd say something like 'a helicopter', they'd say 'go' and you'd come careering down the hill acting the helicopter whilst they tried to nuke you – with fists or feet or squeezy-bottled water – before you got past them. It always ended in tears, in bawling, and sometimes in mothers dragging their kids back inside to behave.

It became the common thing to be forever giving your mother the slip. We had dens and hidey-holes everywhere, and we'd make for them as soon as it looked like we'd be called in, or found out, or sent to bed. In 1976, my favourites were three. One was a concrete ledge under the railway bridge. You had to climb through a wire fence to get to it. It was magical. Brambles always seemed to be growing up the banking of the railway, and we'd scramble down from our ledge in turns –

the others keeping the 'edgy' for adults or trains – and pluck as many of those juicy things as possible. Needless to say, on those hot days your legs would be scratched to bits, so would your arms, and your face would be stained purple. But we'd have armfuls of them up on the ledge with us, and would scream at the tops of our voices as trains roared past, blowing our hair back, its noise drowning us out. There were vertical slats in the wall on the other side of the tracks, and we'd dare each other to skip over there and see if there were any starling's eggs in them. 'I saw two stuckies flying out that one,' you'd say, prompting your pal to a bit of heroic rail-track surfing. Often, when one of us was down there – one of us Brians, or Tams, or Garys – the others would call on you to lay something on top of the track. A brick, or a stick, or an old bit of pram lying against the wall (people were always throwing things down on the railway, like it was a sort of dump). So things would be laid on the track, just out of curiosity, to see what would happen to them when they were hit by the train. We'd cheer from the ledge as the obstacles were glanced out of the way by the train, or just crushed. We'd no idea that this might be dangerous; we thought the train was all-powerful, that it was set on a course and just couldn't be delayed. We'd obviously never heard of derailing.

We got very interested in fire, and our pockets or waistbands would always contain a box of Blue Bells or Swan Vestas or, if pushed, just a couple of strikes out of the box. My pal Mark – who was soon to be my partner in the hunt for books – was at that time an expert fire-raiser. His sister was pretty good too, but Mark was the king. He could always keep a fire going, and he was forever finding interesting things to burn. Bushes would get it, and so would banks of high grass. Our hair and our T-shirts, when I think of it, must've stunk with smoke. I think I may have told my mum, when she asked late in the day what the smell was, that we'd been playing near the bonfire at the dump. There was a dump at the top of Muirside Road, very near us, which often had fires on the go, and kids would gather round to poke it and pile strange things onto it when adults were out of the way. Surprising as it now seems, there were very few accidents. I once saw a boy get a bit of burning plastic on his hand, but it was his own fault. He'd lit the corner of a blue plastic milk crate and hung it up on a fence to burn. Plastic burned very funnily, little bombs of sizzling stuff dipped off in a steady flow. We were all staring at it, speechless, when this boy tried to catch some drips on a stick and instead caught them on the back of his hand.

When I think of that dripping plastic, I think too of a day when Mark and I were messing around on a building site. We were climbing through the rafters of this half-done house – swinging on things, and stealing putty – when we spied these sheets of polythene lying over a pile of hardwood. We got out the Swan Vestas (earlier in the day, we'd exchanged some empty lemonade bottles for them at the newsagent) and started to light it. It went up very quickly, and it was dripping like crazy. The stuff that it was dripping onto was going on fire, and we scarpered. We never found out if the fire raged much, or if some workie came and put it out. But years later, we were sure of one thing: it was the house that my mother lives in today. We moved into it when the burning excitements of childhood had turned into the routine angst of adolescence. It was the same house.

Our childish pursuits that summer were, in a sense, extracurricular. I mean, we had other sides to the day, other enthusiasms. I was often with the girls, skipping and playing peever. The sight of this used to drive some of my brothers daft, they thought this was out and out sissy behaviour. But it was always the way. Whenever I got fed up of the rough and tumble, with setting fires and being with the boys, I'd go off to a corner and make daisy-chains with the lasses. I was never into football, and my brothers were all great at it. But I thought I had the best of both worlds: I could climb and go wrecking with the mob, but also get away into some back garden or swing-park, for a spot of colouring-in, singing, and you-show-me-yours-I'll-show-you-mine with the girls. My favourite days were the ones spent roaming with a gang consisting of boys and girls. Such days had a slightly deranged, Famous-Five-gone-awry feeling about them. And a lot of this time was spent exploring the second of my favourite hideaways: the derelict bits of the local ICI plant.

The explosives factory was bordered by a large expanse of trees, built in among a load of sand-dunes and marshy waste. The trees were supposed to protect the housing estates from the blast in the event of a major accident. The two cooling towers dominated the sky around here in 1976, and we loved the mysterious forest below them. I later found out that the sand was something of a natural resource; its consistency was rare and was used in glass-making, still one of the area's important industries. But at that time it just seemed like a gigantic sandpit to us, and it seemed very much abandoned. To get into the plant you had to crawl – or walk if you were cool enough – across a long black pipe that stretched over a spongy bog beside Todhill Farm, the training centre for Down's syndrome boys. Some of us were quite into birds, we'd found books on them, and you'd see kestrels and owls, and marshland types like grebes, flying in and out of the mysterious world behind the ICI fence. I thought of it first like a prehistoric place, then as an Emerald City, and ultimately as a sort of Gormenghast.

We made our way across at least two hundred yards of pipe, and crawled under the fence, which had pictures of Alsatian dogs tied on, and squiggly symbols that I thought meant 'electricity'. We called the Alsatians Shane, after a dog in our square which was always biting children's fingers through its fence. Once inside ICI, you'd immediately see rabbits running everywhere, and foxes, and sometimes falcons flying in and out of pipes lying up on their sides. The whole place had the appearance of work having been halted only seconds before. There was a special railway inside, which had those little trucks on them that you could make move, two of you, by pressing up and down on the central lever. The trucks often had building materials on them, as if work was in progress. In amongst the trees there were huts covered in netting, which you could go inside. There was paper on the desks, fire extinguishers stood in the corners, and filing cabinets around the edges. There were phones, but when you lifted them up there was no tone. Yes, it all had the feeling of a place abandoned very recently, and in a hurry too.

I never found out what went on there, whether it was still part of the functioning industry there or not, but I never saw anybody working during our little outings. We would go to the top of one of the sand-dunes (it looked like a crater on the moon) and we'd roll down the hills with abandon and pretend to lie dead at the bottom. You got a great view of our houses from up there; you could see the shape of the whole thing. There was once a digger in the middle of the crater, a modern JCB, and it still had keys in the ignition. My school pal David was game for trying to drive it, but it wouldn't move. I only ever saw an adult in there once, and that was a ferocious security guard, who came bounding after us one day as we tried to escape back under the fence, and he threatened to let his Shane (growling on the leash) catch us before we made it onto the pipe. I remember panicking, and wondering whether the dog could keep its balance on the pipe. My pal Arlene froze on the spot. The guard came under and forced us to turn out our pockets. He took away our matches, asked us our names, and said it would be a police matter. We didn't go back to the queer world after that, though we'd sometimes look over from the top of a swing-park chute, or from the top of flats, still wondering what sort of place it actually was.

The third of my secret places takes me a bit beyond 1976. It was a place I'd go to most often alone, when the stuff of the recent past was sparring in my head with a new-found preoccupation with books. It was a place outside of the newer housing schemes, a place that, as much as ICI, made me think of a world that was strange to me, and hard to get to know. It was in the centre of Kilwinning and, to everyone, was a symbol of the old world that the town had a place in long before the ambitions of sixties planning held sway. It was the ruins of Kilwinning Abbey, and, with the old graveyard at its side, it was captivating. The abbey was built by a nobleman called Hugh de Morville in the twelfth century, was inhabited by Cistercian monks from the Continent, and was destroyed during the Reformation. There were symbols carved into the stone in places, and these symbols were said to be Masonic. The Masonic Hall in Kilwinning I knew to be a big deal. It was, like the Orange Lodge round the corner, very well established in the culture of the town. But the Masons' Hall was famous for other reasons; it was the first Lodge in Scotland, and was named the Mother Lodge (No. 0). Alexander Boswell, the son of the more famous James, had been a grandmaster of that Lodge, and so had many of the Earls of Eglinton – the local aristos – whose ruined castle became another of my haunts.

The Masons were very secret; teachers wouldn't answer any of your questions about them in school. They were thought to be very uncatholic. But their mystery and their history would come to fascinate me all the same, and I'd think about those early Masons as I sat on the green at the centre of the ruined abbey, which they were said to have built. The steeple and the knave were still standing, though some of the books I'd read on that green would tell me that the steeple was not the original. At half past five in the morning of 2 August 1814, the top of the great steeple fell onto the green; another portion fell at ten, and the rest was blown down with gunpowder later in the month. Local accounts from that time tell of a general mourning, and a sense of great loss. The steeple is a fixed point to all, and a reminder to many of worlds that long preceded their own. It was rebuilt in the Gothic style, and was as dignified and conspicuous to some of us, coming over to it from our new houses, as it had been to others before. It was hard to read the writing on many of those graves; a lot of them lay flat. I would follow the chiselled script with a finger, and try to make it out. Sometimes you'd see shipping symbols or references, or what seemed like skull-and-crossbones.

The local library was just round the corner, and I began to bring books from there to the abbey some mornings. Now and again, I'd be climbing through the old windows, and clambering over the ruins, waiting for the library to open in the afternoon, to let me have some more. This happened over time, and often

I'd run away from the books to do other things, then come back to them, as if refreshed. I got into dancing, and hoped that one day I could dance in front of people. I thought I could do that, but it might be that I was more interested in the life of dancers as read about in books than actually about the doing of the dance. There were many little temptations, and I spent a long time thinking I might have another sort of life if I found the right how-to manual. But, though it would take a long time to notice it, I was already having another sort of life. I was lazy but books were making me less so. I was determined to get very used to them, and perhaps to let them win me in the end.

A few of us played in these years around the ruined castle of Eglinton, which sat at the centre of a grassy estate on the outskirts of the town. We'd sometimes hang around there, digging and chasing, till the stone got really cold and the sky went orange. Our fits of badness and mischief were somehow tempered by these surroundings, especially if I was with my best friend Mark, who liked science and ghosts, and who was coming to like graveyards and buildings as much as I did. Mark was crazy, and would do anything, but he was a thoughtful boy as well, and we were to become secretive little partners in the search through libraries and museums and markets, in and out of derelict buildings, and along the harbour looking for news and fun. Eglinton Castle had my mind racing. Those grassy banks and ornamental bridges over the frog spawny Lugton River joined those places and things which brought the past to us, and lifted us out of ourselves, out of our sense that all that was living was all that was new. There was a monument at the top of the hill, a spot that marked Robert Burns's rovings over this wood in the company of his sailor friend Richard

Brown. Burns had come to Irvine in 1781 to try and make his living as a flax dresser. The work was hellish.

In the 1950s, a house was being renovated nearby, and the workers found some notebooks in the attic. They were old books, wrapped up, and shrouded in dust. As it turned out, they were the day-books of Dr Fleming, who attended the sick and troubled of the town in the late eighteenth century. There, deep in the run of covered pages, you find an account of visits made in October 1781 to Robert Burns, flax dresser. He had a mysterious sickness, a deep melancholy, and he was attended many times that winter. A Kilwinning man, Robin Cummell, who worked at Eglinton Castle at the time, later remembered Burns's place of employment – now part of the heritage trail – being burnt to the ground. Another man, who left Irvine as a child and went to Canada, came back to the town in old age, and told about the fire at the heckling shop. He remembered, way at the beginning of his memory, standing outside the burning cottage, throwing snowballs into the fire. They were trying to put it out. Burns wrote his 'Dejection: An Ode' during this period, and tried to find other work. Robin Cummell saw Burns at the Wheatsheaf Inn (now the Eglinton Arms) in the High Street, drinking in the regular company of 'Richie Brown, the sailor; Keelivine, the writer; and Tammy Struggles frae the Briggate'. The Irvine of Burns was that of John Galt – full of smuggling, awash with beggary, rousing to the sound of a new and coming commercial world. But it didn't work out for Burns – his own plans for travel to the Americas came unstuck – and he returned to farmwork in south Ayrshire. He would later write in a letter of how those days in Eglinton Park had been inspiring, had warmed him in difficult times, and he credited Richard Brown with two things: with encouraging him to start publishing his poems, and secondly – though other accounts might cause us to doubt that he needed direction – to severally enjoy the pleasures of sex.

As we sat against the castle wall, wearing T-shirts barely two feet in circumference, my friends and I had little thought of such things (publication or sex) though one day, surely, we might think about them both. Burns would become a crucial figure among those writers who helped me to live in my town imaginatively, and though I'm sure he had kinder children than us in mind when he wrote the following, I can't help finding it reminiscent of just some of our later days in Eglinton Park:

> The night was still, and o'er the hill
> The moon shone on the castle wa',
> The mavis sang, while dew-drops hang
> Around her on the castle wa'
>
> Sae merrily they danc'd the ring
> Frae e'enin' till the cock did craw,
> And ay the o'erword o' the spring
> Was: – 'Irvine's bairns are bonie a'!

As you already know, we weren't that bonnie. But the raving Burnsian romance, just as it transformed my sense of our world by making me look at the poet's, still makes me look back, to find pattern and passion among the boiling contradictions of my childhood; to look for the thread, when all might only be arbitrary, accidental, or untelling.

We obviously weren't the first, in that park, to kindle the present with a taper from the past. There were no Lord Eglintons left on that estate when we occupied it, but you'd still hear word of them, and especially of one, Archibald William, the thirteenth Earl, who attempted to revive the splendour of the medieval tournament on that site in August 1839. Men who were driven by romantic excess, by Gothic revivalism, mad at the parsimonious nature of Victoria's coronation, and repulsed by the crude goals of the Industrial Revolution, were keen to seek the nobility of a dead era. They were driven in this craze, of course, by the works of Walter Scott, by the fashion for gathering antiquities – both ancient family names, peerages, and the costumes of chivalry – and there was to be no expense spared. From all over Britain and Europe, from as far as America, they came in feudal dress to celebrate the return of the past. Archery and jousting, banqueting and foolery, the eating of stuffed pigs and the admiration of pageant and the Queen of Beauty, brought over a hundred thousand people to Eglinton's Tournament. The local hotels were packed and the houses of Kilwinning and Irvine were brimming over with visitors. The steam engines of the Glasgow & Ayrshire railway had only been running for six weeks at the time of the Tournament, and they put on special trains to transport the incoming thousands. Ships sailing the Clyde between Glasgow and Ayr – the *Highland Mary*, the *Robert Burns* – made special stops at Ardrossan. Eglinton's Tournament caught the spirit of his age, and it was a spirit hypnotized by the glamour of an age long gone.

You might say that a vivid, essential moment in the making and unmaking of civilization occurred in that park. It was a grand fantasy of improvement, showing, as it happened, how the past can both corrupt and enlighten the present. The official guest of honour was Louis Napoleon, the Knight Visitor, and the lists were fought by such as the Earl of Craven, the Marquess of Waterford, and Viscount Glenlyon, all supported by esquires, men-at-arms, standard-bearers, and the like. At the head of all this, in torrential rain, stood the Lord of the Tournament, the thirteenth Earl of Eglinton, in a suit of armour all coloured gold and blue. The rain came down, and ruined the entire event. Hundreds ran for cover, the games were abandoned, and mud covered everything. Eglinton's money continued to dwindle ever afterwards, and he died fairly young, with a great reputation as the man who had tried to make the world new by reviving the past.

In my time, the park was lush and the towers were broken down to one. Sometimes it still rained. There was little to bring back the past, we thought, beyond what could be gleaned from books. The streets in our new town, though, were named after all those noble families and ancient feudal haunts. Our squares – our Ardmillans, and Kelburns, and Garallans – seemed nothing but new, though those names pointed to the stories of others who'd somehow gone before. Our minds were slowly opening up: we lived among the missing and the dead, though only the gathering of years to ourselves would help us to remark upon that. But every day of that time, and for disconnected reasons, we grew aware of it a little more, and a little more.

WE EVENTUALLY STOPPED looking for Sandy that hot summer of 1976. There was no more word of him, and it seemed that he might just have vanished into thin air. But that was never going to do as an explanation, especially after the events of October the same year, when another person, this time a young woman, went missing from a bus stop in the centre of town. Tricia Black was twenty-two, and she lived at

10 Dykes Place in Saltcoats. She left home on Friday 8 October for a night at the dancing. She met up with friends, some of them workmates, and they went to a few pubs, then to the Meadow Club, where you could dance. She stayed out that night, at the house of one of the girls, and left to go home some time the next afternoon. She was last seen at a bus stop opposite the Turf Hotel at 5 p.m. on Saturday; some said in the company of a man. There was no sighting of her on any bus, nobody saw her in any other club or pub or public place. She was at the bus stop, then she vanished.

When Janet Black hadn't seen her daughter by Sunday night, having made some calls to Tricia's friends, she called the police and reported her missing. She'd last heard from her later on the Friday night, when she called to say she'd be staying out. Where was she? Everybody thought it was strange; she wouldn't just go off like that. She seemed quite happy; she didn't even have any stuff with her. What was happening? The police began searching and interviewing and putting out appeals for assistance. Tricia was 5'3"; she was of medium build; dyed black hair – quite short. She had a fresh complexion; wore a low-cut cream-coloured dress and a short fur jacket trimmed with dark leather. Her shoes were brown, and she was carrying a small brown handbag. Most people who'd danced with her the night before, who'd been out with her recently, were spoken to. But nothing. Then they began to comb the bed of the River Irvine.

The search went on for weeks, and on 30 October, in the water near Campbell's Railway Bridge, her handbag was found. The bag was weighted down with stones from the railway line. This is about a mile from where she was last seen, on the other side of Irvine Moor. The entire area was turned over, but there was no sign of Tricia. The handbag was the only thing. There was lots in the papers; investigators were baffled and very suspicious. But it got to the point where nothing more would be done, where there was really nothing more to look at. The disappearance of Tricia Black entered a kind of shock into the community, but it was one that didn't reach children in the way that Sandy's had. You'd see adults talking about it more than children; it had something different about it, but it was hard to understand. We knew that children could get lost (children are forever being told that) and we knew other things, but we thought adults couldn't. We'd heard stories about Glasgow, we'd watched *Starsky & Hutch* on the telly, and we knew that people could kill people. Is that what it meant? Not lost, but killed? It wasn't straight in our heads. Children might be taken away in vans, but not adults? Adults could find their way home, unless someone stopped them? It just wasn't clear.

A month after this, the news was full of the disappearance of Mrs Renee Macrae and her three-year-old son Andrew. They had gone missing, and her BMW had been found burnt out at the side of a road twelve miles south of their home in Inverness. There was no sign of them in the car. Police thought that Mrs Macrae had been planning to go to visit her sister, Morag Govans, in Ayrshire. But she never arrived there. Mr Macrae ran a building firm, and he put up a reward of £1,000 for any information leading to their discovery. Police asked that anyone who'd seen the car – registration number JAS 219P – between noon and 10 p.m. on the Friday of the pair's disappearance should come forward. Renee was separated from her husband, but they still spoke. She didn't seem especially anxious the week before; no one could think of a reason why she might want to go. Digging went on all over the area, hundreds of statements were taken, and police divers searched in freezing lochs and rivers. Reports came from the public, reports of a car having been fleetingly sighted in a lay-by near where the BMW was found; others thought they saw Renee a day or two before her disappearance in the company of a man with a zapata moustache. Posters were put up all over, with pictures of Renee and Andrew, and the words 'Where are they now?' printed underneath. Detective Chief Superintendent Ian Cameron, head of the Northern Constabulary CID, had hundreds of officers working on the case. 'The search for Mrs Macrae will go on,' he said, 'this inquiry will not be closed until we find this woman and child.'

My mother was concerned about this case. She remembers seeing pictures of the little boy's bike in the front garden, and worrying. But there was something else. Within a few days of the initial reports of their disappearance, there were other pictures in the paper, pictures of a man she recognized. It was William McDowell. He was the man with the briefcase, the one who used to whistle on his way up Bathgate Street, the one my mother would see from the window. She was sure it was Mr McDowell – the good man, the fine husband. That was him. The papers reported that Mr McDowell had been having a clandestine affair with Renee Macrae, the wife of his boss. It was the police, in the course of their investigations, who uncovered the affair, and Mr Macrae immediately sacked him from his firm (MacDowell, the man with the briefcase, was the firm's accountant). He said that he and Renee had a secret code of telephone rings. They used the code when ringing each other's houses, when trying to speak to each other without the intervention of a third party. McDowell had heard the familiar rings, he said, two days after the disappearance of Renee and Andrew. Then he heard it again, the week after that, when police were interviewing him in his house. Mr McDowell said he knew nothing of Renee and her son's disappearance. It had nothing to do with him, and the police – after a series of questions – had no reason to suspect differently.

Renee and Andrew have never been found. All clues led nowhere, and the case remains officially open. My mother shook her head over the news, as if in disbelief, at the seemingly impossible vanishing of that nice-looking woman and her lovely boy. She thought about the smart man from Bathgate Street, as well, and wondered what had happened to him, or was happening to him now. It all seemed so long ago, and their lives had gone so differently, or in most ways they seemed to have done. As my mother stood with me at that window in Bathgate Street, with her older children happy around her, watching the young man striding so confidently up the road down below, she could hardly have known how their lives would go. We'd move out there, looking to find life, and there we'd find it. But not on its own. Growing up, and growing away from Glasgow, would be about trying to cut your losses, but always finding there are new ones just around the corner, right next to the gains. My family all grew up together, we were really all children together. Personally, I know I was never the same after 1976. That year gave me an idea of some of the things that could happen in life; it raised questions. The disappearances of that year became tied, in my mind, to fears and wonderings, hopes for the future and curiosities about the past. Immediately after that year, there would be books, and more life, and more sense. Those houses that had been built for us, those entire worlds, would grow increasingly less new; people would die in those houses where no one had died before, life would run out in the usual way, and layers of wallpaper would grow on the walls. We'd fill out our lives, and our jumpers, and in time would move away ourselves. But I'll not forget the importance of those who did not, those who stay frozen but undead in 1976. They are the missing – and in that year they stood over my own, growing, private sense of what it meant to be visible and alive.

Book Two
THE MISSING

MISPERS

IT WAS A SUNDAY morning, and the minister strode past me with a Labrador. 'That looks like a contented spot,' he said, dog and dog-collar glistening. I sat in the middle of a little wood, just to the side of Kenilworth Chapel in East London, on 9 October 1994. The church looked closed and unattended. Around me, in tangles of ivy and nettles and scrub, lay hundreds of dilapidated gravestones. They sloped every which way, and off into the distance, across a wide open ground beneath the Beckton flyover.

The graveyards in English cities, especially in the east of those cities, are nearly always wasted and terrible. In Scotland, the tombstones are made to stand up; and the grass is most often cut and weeded. I was fairly shocked the first time I saw a London graveyard – in Walthamstow, I remember. It had nothing to do with the decorous, landscaped dead-parks of recent memory: it was a place where riot and decay ruled. It looked like a spot where time was having its way.

I sat on a stone, bent over a piece of paper. I was copying down the inscriptions on some of the tombs. As I was doing so, two boys – around or about ten – nipped between the graves just a little off to the right. One of them wore a West Ham top; the other was a flash of yellow. Their missiles (clods of dirt and pebble-dash) would come from nowhere and bounce off the tombs still standing. You'd hear giggles, and see some yellow, then a stripe of claret; they'd peep for a second, then disappear. The more I ignored them, the braver they got. They started letting out little hollers, rinky-dink battle-charges, but I sat still. I was laughing a bit by this time, and they obviously knew I knew about them. Eventually, they got within one or two tombstones, and I looked up from the page. 'What is it?' I said. 'Cunt,' they said, running away – tumbling through a wall of ivy as if the whole world was after them. They ran and ran, and eventually their great colours blinked out in the distance.

The stone to my right was Africa-shaped and fringed with damp moss. Most of the writing was gone now. *Also Rebecca Askham, mother of the above* I could make out. And then: *who died October 1st 1903. Aged 50 years.* The nettles around the bottom were at the top of their power; I knew from experience that those white buds were significant. They stood for pain. The stone on my other side was in memory of *Frank Cyril Nicholson, who died January 13th 1897, aged 14 years.* It was a cool day, very quiet at times, then some horn or deep engine on the dual carriageway would break in. Frank Cyril died after fourteen years; died, it seems, of natural causes. His death must have been very sad, but was probably not mysterious. His was a named loss. The cause was known, the end was marked, his spot was here, and was in a manner of speaking sacred. I sat thinking about all this, feeling the breeze well enough, and considering the ornate script carved below Frank Cyril's dates: *In the midst of life*, it said, *we are in death*.

I had a stick, and with other people, later that day, I searched the long field of stones at Kenilworth Chapel for traces of a missing boy. Daniel Handley, aged nine, had been missing from his home on the Windsor Park Estate since the previous Sunday. As I made my way down the field, losing sight of the others, I grew more and more uneasy. This was the largest patch of scrub near to Daniel's home. I turned over in my head the various things that could have happened. I looked through the undergrowth, poking with the stick, and I reached a point almost under the flyover itself. The traffic noise was now thunderous, and the grass seemed longer than at any other point. My breath was quite short. I stood thinking. What could have happened? I looked up at the motorway. It had those overhead signs, the ones with flashing arrows.

The place was loud, and the grass felt spongy. There were brambles growing up the banking at the side of the carriageway. It felt wrong to walk in this deep grass. Not just unsafe. Wrong. As I made my way through the field, looking into the grass and under bushes for signs of the boy – hoping that I'd find nothing

– I found it hard to keep my footing. The light at the top of Canary Wharf blinked just over the other side, and the sun was high above. The tower looked broad and massive, and its windows gleamed like the vicar's collar. Daniel Handley was missing, and we were there trying to find him. We were there, walking on graves, trying to find the missing boy.

The previous day I'd gone to Daniel's house. The Windsor Park Estate sits very near the Royal Albert Dock, just on the north bank of the Thames beside East Ham and Barking. It's an area made up of newish housing schemes, heavy roads, flyovers, industrial parks, expansive malls and playing-fields. At the beginning of the estate, on the corner of Winsor Terrace and Woolwich Manor Way, about five minutes from Daniel's house, there's a giant building site. There are mounds of rubble and dirt, roving dumpers, stacks of brick, packs of cement and pyramids of Cellophane-wrapped pipe. There's a giant sign at the edge of the rubble: ANOTHER PRESTIGIOUS HOTEL DEVELOPMENT FOR WHITBREAD MEDWAY INNS, CONSTRUCTED BY DEAN & BOWES LTD, HUNTINGDON. The site was fenced off, though I managed to have a look around without much trouble. It was mostly empty, with hard-hatted workmen doing their thing in this or that corner. The ground was uneven, it was full of holes, but I guessed the police had already considered that.

A large Asda superstore stands across the road, with bus stops planted outside. Daniel worked here as a bag filler. This was how he earned pocket money, and he was a well-known face around the area. He was out playing on his BMX bike the day he disappeared. It was silver and had no saddle. Like many kids his age, he would use the kerbs and ramps around the scheme, and the empty industrial estates just beyond it, to practise stunts on his bike. He was out doing that sort of thing on Sunday 2 October, and he played for some time at the house of a friend, but he failed to return home afterwards. He set out late in the afternoon, but had somehow not made it. That evening, two boys found an abandoned silver BMX on Eisenhower Drive, round the corner from Daniel's house. The boys made off with it, and took it back to their home in Clapton, where they wiped it down, and thought to keep it. When they heard of the missing boy, though, they gave the bike to the police, who found that it was Daniel's.

Daniel was the fourth of Maxine Williams's five boys. In April 1994 Maxine had left the family home she shared with her husband David Handley in Newark Knok, and taken the kids to live at the house of her boyfriend Alex Joseph, at Lobelia Close in Beckton. Daniel went to Beckton Cross Primary School, and was one of those kids who'd talk to anyone. He already had girlfriends, and was one of the dare-devils at school, one of the live wires, one of the minor pushers-and-shovers. He had, in the usual manner for the younger of several boys, a fair amount of brotherly reputation to live up to, or to live down. Some of his brothers were thought to be quite flash, and to be fairly unshy when it came to the business of standing up for things. His schoolmates talked to me of the Handleys as of one of those families who can easily absorb trouble, and who could dish it out just as easily. The mother's boyfriend Alex is black, and even in an area as multi-racial as East London can be, there was a certain amount of prejudice in the local area about the fact of his living in Lobelia Close with a white woman and her children. People talked about them, and they did so, it seems, even before Daniel disappeared.

He'd been wearing a red boiler suit that day, which had the

word 'Racing' stitched onto the left pocket. Underneath he had a green jumper. He also wore brown boots. The lake at the top of Beckton District Park had been dredged with special equipment; the gasworks and sewage-treatment plant to the east had been searched thoroughly; warehouses and parks had been gone into; and door-to-door calls were under way all week. I turned into the close the day they were due to start digging in the garden. There were television vans parked along the sides, and journalists were lining up behind the police tape, anxious for photos and news. A guy from the *Mail on Sunday* stood wrapped in one of those long overcoats. He was biting his nails, worrying about having missed the early-morning press conference. At first, there was only a solitary female police officer guarding the house. The tape stretched across the road in such a way that people who lived on either side of the Handley house had to run underneath it. Most of those going by were kids, and they zoomed right under on their BMXs and racers; they did it repeatedly, just for a laugh. They were showing off for the journalists, and were obviously trying to wind up the lady officer.

The man from the *Mail on Sunday* walked round and round the close, chapping on all the doors, getting really steamed up. He didn't seem to be taking very serious notes: every time he heard something interesting – and often when he heard something not – he'd pull out his mobile phone and call his news desk. He'd repeat it to them hastily, clearly experiencing some sort of deadline fever. The policewoman told me she thought he was 'facetious', and sort of rolled her eyes when the *Daily Star* walked up. Even amidst the solemnity and dead seriousness of this stake-out, there was something very funny about the man from the *Star*. Everyone looked at him. He stalked up and down the pavement, sucking one fag after another down to nothing, his head bowed with the weight of two or three cameras. His hair was very short at the front, very long at the back, and greasy all over; his suit was shiny, and the trousers sagged at half-mast. He had a thin moustache and he walked like a loopy pigeon.

He pointed to a little Asian boy who played just in front of the tape. 'Is your mum in, sonny?' he asked. The boy nodded. 'Can you ask her to come out here a minute?' The boy ran inside. A few seconds later an adult arm appeared at the door, but only long enough to pull it shut and turn the key in the lock. 'That,' says the star from the *Star*, 'is a definite no.'

'Why don't you stand on the back wall?' says a blonde woman in dark glasses.

'Tried that.'

'Eight of them, there's eight of them digging in the garden,' says an older guy, a producer type, who had just stepped out of a red Volvo. 'I think one of the snappers has got them at it.'

Maxine Williams and Alex Joseph, Daniel's mother and her boyfriend, were in a DSS safe-house during the search. One of the neighbours, a middle-aged white man backed up by his wife, takes the opportunity to speak with the assembled press. 'You, from where, yes, BBC South & East, oh yes. And you, Sky? ITV? No, ITN. OK.' He identifies himself as a close neighbour and then starts. He has the air of someone familiar with the plot. He emphasizes certain things, he makes a few tough points about how one should live in a community, and then he hammers home a series of assertions that you wouldn't care to hear. I couldn't print them, and the TV journalists knew – as he spoke – that they wouldn't be able to broadcast them either. Halfway through his spiel, I saw the guy from *Newsroom South-East* gently switch off his camera.

I stayed by the fence for a while after the other people had gone. I wanted to talk with the kids. The Asian woman from next door eventually turned the key. She came over to me, and asked if there had been any more news. I gave her what I had. She offered me coffee, and told me I could look out of her bedroom window if I wanted. It was right over the spot where they were digging. I thanked her, but didn't go in. The police were coming in and out from the yard, wearing blue jumpers and white gloves. CID were doing the rounds of the houses, dressed in grey suits and carrying clipboards. A crowd of small boys had gathered around the tape.

'Give's a fag,' said one.

'You're too young,' said I.

'Am I fuck. I've smoked for ages.'

'Age are you?'

'Nine,' he said, pulling a ten-pack from his pocket, and lighting one up behind a tiny cupped hand.

'Same age as Daniel,' I said.

'He smoked as well. He used to go out with my big sister. What do you think has happened to him?'

'I don't know. What do you think?' At this point the others butted in. Two of them were thirteen, and one other nine. They gave me their theories, told me all about their parents' suspicions, and reeled out the local gossip. The little one was still swaggering about with his fag, clowning and blowing smoke-rings. They talked about Alex, about how good a fighter he was. 'He's a bodybuilder,' said one of the thirteens.

'Brilliant muscles like that,' said another, pulling up a sleeve of his T-shirt.

'Can we talk into your tape-recorder?' shouted Jason, the miniature smoker. I gave it to them, and they started barking into it – sentences and short stories all to do with such and such among them being 'dickless' or 'a virgin' or 'pricks' and 'bastards'.

'Daniel is just like any other kid,' said the uncamera-shy neighbour with the jittering wife. 'These children were often kept away from school. I'd see it, and I'd want to complain. I knew something wasn't right.' One of the kids told me that Alex's mum was the funniest person alive. She gave them money; you'd see her staggering across Lobelia Close with a can of Superlager, her dog Lady limping at her back.

'She's brilliant,' said Jason, handing back my recorder. Just then, an ice-cream van – Tony's Super Whip – came jangling down the street, and they all went after it.

For six months or so, Daniel Handley's whereabouts was unknown. He was yet another missing child, and most people had given up hope of ever finding him, or of ever finding him well. They weren't to be proved wrong on the last bit. The boy's body, still clad in his red boiler suit, was found in a wooded area outside Bristol in April. He'd been murdered, and placed in a rough grave, covered in leaves and dirt. That's where he'd lain all those months.

The police spoke of a paedophile ring, and revealed details of Operation Oyster, an attempt by officers to close in on an East London gang. Witnesses came forward. A woman in Bristol recalled seeing someone just like Daniel, a little boy in red, in the company of three men in a café. The boy seemed quite happy, quite cheerful, and the men were friendly enough too. But, for whatever reason, a clear picture of the group remained in her head. A boy like Daniel was spotted again in Bristol one Sunday in November. Two men were holding his hands tight, walking him down the street. The boy seemed a bit distressed.

The child who rode down Eisenhower Drive on his saddleless bike that bright afternoon in October had encountered something dreadful on his way. The police have issued photofits and descriptions, and called for every sort of assistance. They are waiting for more responses and, in the meantime, have brought down the files on missing local children.

THERE ARE ALL sorts of missing. The world is full of missing persons, and their numbers increase all the time. The space they occupy lies somewhere between what we know about the ways of being alive and what we hear about the ways of being dead. They wander there, unaccompanied and unknowable, like shadows of people. Of course, the person named on the birth certificate will either have a life or they will not. They may be alive somewhere, and unknown. Or they may be dead somewhere, and unknown. The situation – for a while, perhaps in some cases for all time – is that we just don't know. The person missing cannot be brought into focus, their presence, their person, derived from their birth, can no longer be verified. They may be out there; they must be somewhere. They may have covered themselves in modern life, or modern life may have covered them. Whatever else, they are ill-apparent. They may now be somebody else; they may be simply (or not so simply) living in another place; they may be seeable, and driving past your window now. Or there might be something sinister; the name they were given, the life that is theirs, may have been scratched out. They may be unseeable, they may have been killed, and the body – every person's private evidence of themselves – may be concealed in the earth, or obliterated, leaving nothing behind.

Some people deliberately go, finding a new life and identity, remaining concealed among the everyday, shrouded in normality. Such people, like one man I know, are often on the run from debts and bad marriage, from disappointment and depression at being who they are. Brian had had enough of Brian, and he turned against – or away – from Northumberland, and his house, his family, and the preconceptions of his friends and colleagues. He left Brian behind, and became Jeremy. He taught himself new things, became a college lecturer somewhere else in Britain, and he founded a whole new self – one, he says, more like the self he was in the early days, before Brian became an institution. For those left in Northumberland, the years have passed, and they have sometimes been years slow with confusion and guilt. They thought Brian was probably dead or abroad. He'd succumbed to severe depression, perhaps, and something bad had happened to him. He was a missing person, and there was always to be pain and doubt around his name. For Jeremy, the person he used to be is just a memory. He knows that his family miss him, this formerly very apparent, very present, very changeless man called Brian. But there is no going back.

There are times when an individual's disappearance will quickly be remarked upon, where reports will be filed and searches instigated. Such cases are ones where the missing person is thought to be in some way vulnerable; cases where the person is missed, where their absence is noted, and where foul play will be suspected if no other explanation offers itself quite quickly. People who live within sight of family, friends, doctors, and neighbours – those who are actually seen by other people – will not go missing very easily. But they *can* go missing. And it is their numbers, the legions of the missed, who feature in the statistics. In 1994 the Metropolitan Police Missing Persons Bureau was notified of 23,528 missing persons. These are the reported ones, the missed, and there is no saying just where they are, though we might begin to say something of who they are.

I DID AS I was told, and turned into the Bourne Estate at the Leather Lane end. The place was tidy, well swept, with a large, solid arch at the opening to each court. The guy in front of me kicked his dog. As if from nowhere, a little army of pensioners in overalls swooped in on him. 'I saw yer do that yesterday,' said one of them, 'and if I catch yer doin' it again, it's the police, right?' The guy shrugged, denied it, and made off. 'Cruel bastard,' shouted one of the ladies. She was standing like a set of scales, balancing two shopping bags a few inches off the ground on either side of her. 'Somebody should bloody kick him!'

Most of the doors had those stickers on them, the ones that say 'No Collectors' or 'No Salesmen'. Others had bright orange notices advertising the local Neighbourhood Watch. I had been here a few days before, and Mr Bennett was out. On that day, there was a funeral going on downstairs, and the street was full of wreaths and flowers. The court was quiet, though full of people, and the cockney bustle of Leather Lane market seemed as if it was miles away. People, mainly elderly people, were staring down from verandas all the way up the block. One or two held hankies, or towels. The dead man's name was writ large in the middle of some of the wreaths. As I made my exit, I almost tripped over a couple of young razor-cuts, bombing round the corner in their black ties.

So this was my second visit to see Mr Bennett. He buzzed me up, and came to the door with no shirt on. I followed him into the kitchen. A lumpy cat padded between us, and found a place under the sink, as we sat down at the table to talk. Mr Bennett used to be the caretaker on this part of the estate, and he knew all about it. 'Big changes round here,' he said.

'What kind?'

'Oh, a lot of people dead, a helluva lot of people dead, and the young people are all away,' he said, blinking. We sat the whole time covered in blue light, which came out of a small TV, sitting on top of the fridge. Mr Bennett had lost his job, and he lived alone, having split from his wife many years ago. It took us a while, with one thing and another, to get to the subject of Billy. I asked him to go back to the beginning.

'Billy was born in the London Hospital, Whitechapel,' he said, 'in 1966. We were living, his mother and me, and his sister, just down the road then.' Things, it seems, were all right, and the seventies passed pretty normally. It was in the eighties that things started to go wrong. Mr Bennett split up with his wife, Billy started hanging around with a different crowd, taking LSD, and getting depressed. There was no work for him. Since leaving school, he hadn't had a job of any sort, though most people say he wasn't that interested in doing work, even if it had been there for the taking. He started staying in his room, drinking a few lagers, listening to his sounds, and he did this a lot more after he broke up with his girlfriend. The LSD was doing him no good; he was taken into a psychiatric ward at the Royal Free Hospital many times, but he'd always leave, and go to a friend's house, where he felt safer. Lowell was his friend.

In December 1985, Billy was planning to get away for a

holiday. He was very unhappy, and he was due to appear in court on a charge of theft. He'd stolen a pair of gloves from a local shop. He went to Tenerife the night before the court date. Lowell drove him to the airport on 19 December, and he told Billy to lie low for a while, take it easy. He wasn't well, and he was prone to a little trouble, so maybe he needed to just chill out somewhere, and Tenerife was good for that. Billy said goodbye, and got on the plane. In Tenerife, he bumped into a pal called Tony, who was over there with his girlfriend. They met a few times. He wasn't looking well, the couple said later. He seemed out of it – high on something – and, at one point, he said he'd lost his passport and everything. Then he disappeared.

Checks were made to see if he was in prison, or hospital, or drowned. Only one thing turned up around that time – a rumour, something about Billy being chased by certain unknown officials with guns. Billy was reported missing. Investigations by Interpol, detectives, family members, and Home Office officials followed, but there has been no word. In a reported missing case like Billy's, it emerges, over time, that there is more than one vulnerable person involved. Where the missing person is being missed, it is usually the case that some-one visible, someone back home, will be going through a sort of hell, a misery of endless doubt and speculation. Mr Bennett is one of these, one of the missers, whose life has been stalled and damaged by his son's disappearance. I kept trying to talk to him about himself, about his life, but he quickly reverted back to the details and possibilities surrounding Billy's case. 'You think you know your kids, but sometimes you don't,' he said. 'I thought he would have got in touch. When he was a little kid, he'd come in the house and immediately it'd be "Where's Mummy? Where's Mummy?", and his mother is a wonderful woman, the best in the world, you know?'

'Was he close to her?' I asked.

'Well, you know, he didn't show it. The only thing that could've disturbed him – and I'm not saying this is the case – is his mum, she took up with this bloke about the same time. I would say – and it's my opinion – that that did affect him. He said to one of his mates, after I'd left, it's only for a little while, then he'll be back.'

I braced myself, and looked at the telly for a second, before I said anything else. 'Do you think he was suicidal?'

Mr Bennett looked at me. 'He once said to Lowell he'd like to top himself. And it runs in my family. My dad committed suicide, but my dad was a sick man. My mother died at thirty-seven. He lost his wife. I was the eldest of five, you know? His mother's brother, too, he did himself in.'

'What's it like,' I say, 'thinking that?'

'It's mental torture,' he says, 'that's what it is, mental torture.'

'When you think of Billy, what age do you picture him at – do you think of him at nineteen, or as a twenty-eight-year-old man?'

'Yes,' he said, 'I think about him as a nineteen-year-old boy, 'cause that's the way he was last time I saw him. I can't imagine him as a man. You see, I was fourteen when my mother died, and then when my wife and me split up, I was affected, but this was the worst of all. I'm not happy, I'll never be happy till I find out what happened to him. I'd be a different person then, I really would.' He says he finds himself grasping at anything, any bit of hope. Someone phoned the Missing Persons Helpline to say that Billy was in the Foreign Legion. Then someone else said it, though the date of entry was different. The Legion has no record, it says, of a Billy Bennett, nor of someone called Victor Sexton, the name being used by the man identified as Billy by one of the anonymous telephone callers.

Mr Bennett went to see an old Foreign Legion corporal, who showed him and his wife some photographs from Legion magazines. One of them looked very like Billy, both parents agreed. The man in the photo was identical to him. When they went back to the corporal's house a while later, they couldn't find the photo again. There was another one, though, another photo, and it looked like Billy too.

Mr Bennett brought me the photograph. I set it beside other pictures of Billy, and it did have a sort of resemblance. It showed a young soldier lying on the ground with a helmet on, holding a rifle, one eye closed, taking his aim. Brown hair, blue eyes, 5'10"? Maybe. The corporal said it wasn't Billy: the guy in the photo was German, he was younger than Billy was. Billy's father still thinks it might be him; he's a bit haunted by this grainy picture, this dark soldier, this double of his own son.

Mr Bennett is fifty. When I asked him if he was a different sort of teenager from Billy, he said he was much the same, and reminded me that things were very different then. He got married at nineteen, and all he thought of having, all he wanted, was a wife and kids and a flat in London. His daughter is single, and she lives in a residential Gospel hall; he still sees her, and his wife, now and then, but all of them have their own, separate lives. We sat quiet for a minute. The cat was ripping up a storm on the hall carpet, and it was pitch black outside.

'I was born in Glasgow,' he said. 'My granny lived in Tambowie Street, in Anniesland. It's probably not there now, but I'd love to go back and see. I've not been there since I was a boy, but I can remember the dead-end of the street; there was a place you could steal coal; there was a railway there.

Closes they called them, closes this side, closes that side' – he began drawing it in the air with his hand – 'and an arch, just over here. That would be the place I'd most like to go to now.' We shook hands at the door. Mr Bennett seemed so much older than he was. You could see he missed his son, just as he still missed his wife, missed his past, and maybe sometimes missed his work, too. When I stepped outside, all I could hear was young voices, young shouts and hoots, echoing round the stairwells of the Bourne Estate. Some voices came too from a fenced-off playground in the middle, where jubilant shouts at the scoring of a goal, and oaths at the letting of one in, mingled and clashed under the yellow floodlights.

THERE ARE THOUSANDS of missing persons in Britain whose disappearance is never reported. They fall out of troubled homes, Special Care, and approved schools every other day. Under the new regulations, many people with mental health bother are decanted out of hospitals and into the streets and night-shelters that now act as a sort of security net for them. Such people – often voluntarily at first – lose sight of all that they have been before. Many you talk to can't remember much or anything about who they used to be. Runaways, amnesiacs, schizophrenics, victims of abuse. Every year, thousands burst – or are thrust – out of what community they have known; they take up their lives anonymously, often on the streets of Britain's bigger cities. Most of them lose touch; benefits are often unclaimed; relatives are gladly left behind or were never there in the first place. These are the unmissed, and it is possible that over two hundred thousand people at any given time in Britain can be described this way.

Whether missed or not, the common condition of all the missing (apart from their being out of sight) is that their documentary lives stop at the point they disappear. This termination, in fact, explains what it means to be a missing person in a country such as Britain. From birth, something like a small maelstrom of official paper swirls round your body, defining your human relations (birth certificates, marriage certificates); outlining your religious life (baptisms, Holy Communions, Confirmations); describing your physical progression (medical records); the history of your teeth (dental records); your education (report cards, school files); giving evidence of your social life (club minutes, membership cards); defining your financial status (National Insurance contributions, tax returns, wage slips); your professional life (employment records, application forms, job appraisal reports); your mental or custodial history (psychiatric reports, social work papers, prison records); your domestic routines (phone records, gas bills, newspapers delivered); and hundreds of other extant documents relating to the conduct of your life. These are bits of paper long forgotten by you, and by most people. These official records (to say nothing of private documents, letters, and diaries) give a very full account of who you are, and what your movements have been over the course of your life.

Ours is a very written-down sort of life; it can't easily be erased, nor can the binding power of ongoing records be easily snapped. Many of these records follow you wherever you go, and, in the normal run of things, they can cause you to be traced very quickly. A missing person has – for one of a variety of reasons I'm turning over – severed, or been severed from, their written life. They are not cashing cheques in their own name, they are not drawing benefit or earning money through their NI number, they are not paying tax, they are not visiting a doctor or a dentist in possession of their files, and, as police investigators quickly find out during a search, they are not regularly matching the pattern of what is known about them. You can change your identity, but it is not just a matter of going to another town and calling yourself Jeremy. It is a gigantic undertaking: a trail of subterfuge and avoidance of past documents leads away from the who-you-were to the who-you-are-now. This scenario mostly applies to the non-vulnerable missing – that's to say, people who may deliberately go missing for reasons of their own. It applies less to the unmissed, or to vulnerables whose disappearance is much more sinister. There is no big deal, for them, in turning away from the documents of the past. For runaways and abuse victims and schizophrenics, those documents are not binding in the way they were for Brian from Northampton. They are unmissed, and nobody is making the connections: they never had cheque-books, they never had work, and they will have all sorts of names to offer to hostel workers and doctors if they ever see them. Children who disappear, the most vulnerable category of all, have no big documentary lives anyway, they just have lives. There is no tracing them. When children go missing, there can only be the possibility of foul play, a strange accident, or a stranger.

The police call them mispers. They are everywhere and nowhere; in the world and out of it; each of them different and each the same. Mispers. In a missing person inquiry, the work will usually be coordinated by the local force, and by the local CID. It will be them who conduct door-to-door enquiries, who organize missing posters, tracker dogs, ground searches, street work, and publicity. In some places, especially in built-up places, there will be police stations that employ a

special officer for work on missing persons cases. The job is
not just about finding people, it is also a matter of identifying
people who have been found dead in the local area. The dead
will be people who died alone, men and women whom nobody
seems to know. The missing persons officers have a double job
to do: finding people to fit names, and finding names to fit
people.

PC GARRARD IS the officer responsible for mispers at Limehouse, in East London. The station is one of the old kind, with
a stone front and the date, 1888, carved over the door. At
certain times of the day, a fat shadow engulfs the front of
the building. This bit of midday dusk falls in the shape of the
Canary Wharf Tower, which is just over the way, on the other
side of the Docklands Light Railway. As I walked towards the
Limehouse Station steps, I looked over at the DLR trains
coming and going. It was amazing the way those trains could
go, surfing along on their electrified tracks without need of
a driver. The driver's seat was empty. That would be pretty
uncomfortable, I thought, pretty scary. It reminded me of something in the past, something I'd seen on one of those pre-school
afternoons in the house with my mum. It was a film called
Ghost Train, one of those British pictures featuring Arthur
Askey and a band of posh-spoken English thespians. They were
all stuck in a sinister railway station on a stormy night, they'd
been warned by someone with the usual glittering eye that the
place was haunted. They stayed, Askey made bad jokes, gad-
ding up and down with his big bum, and the driverless ghost-
train came screaming through the station, putting the fear of
death into those who watched it go. I'd seen it on afternoon

TV that first time. I could see it as clear, and as straight up, as I could see the doors of Limehouse police station. The light coming through the blinds, and beaming out of the TV, was twinkly with unsettled dust and particles of Mr Sheen. The ghost train rumbled off the edge of a cliff. I was cross-legged in pyjamas, and I'd never seen anything so terrible in my life.

Daniel Handley's face stared out from a missing poster just inside the door. I went past it and into the canteen, where PC Garrard came to meet me a coffee or two later. He was obviously one of those long-standing all-rounders; someone who could be efficient and popular at the same time, and without much visible effort. As we walked through the corridors to reach his office, there was a slap or a word for everyone. He'd swing on open doors and settle a point of business over here, swat a junior there; joking and trouble-shooting all the way. Preterhumanly cheerful, and clearly very good at what he did. And you feel that no one resents that sort of being good, they just envy it, and feel a bit lucky to be close by.

The Met press officer who follows us is one of the newer breed. He's friendly in a PR sort of way, more courteous than friendly. He's slightly afraid of real conversation. Garrard knows how to deal with outsiders like me, he knows how to bring you in, just so far as will do for him, and then release you. He's been with journalists, you can tell, and he knows how the thing goes. The newer breed are constantly on the look out for stitch-ups and mistakes in etiquette. They do a good enough job, but they do it rather nervously, often with a fastidiousness quite out of sync with the way people – people like police and journalists anyway – will enter into some sort of common exchange. Garrard understands the mutual aspect, and is afraid of no one. There's nothing to hide from, there's nothing to be officious about, there's just the facts, and his experience of the facts. There will, of course, be factual information that is classified, and he'll tell you that and move on from it. The PR guy will repeat the injunction, as if you're unlikely to understand why certain material in an investigation must be secret. Garrard proceeds in his own way: he knows the drama, he knows what the story could be, he knows where the detail is, and he is quite aware of what I'm looking for. He laughs a lot. The PR sits tight: he is fully taken up with what the story is not.

'Let's see if we can't find a drink in here!' says Garrard, fumbling blindly in a cupboard. We're not in his usual office, so he starts us off with a few gags about the secret habits of policemen. He trills with laughter, I snigger away, and the PR chews his bottom lip. 'You happy?' he says to me.

'Mm.'

'OK. I'm PC Chris Garrard. I've been at Limehouse for over twenty-four years, the first fifteen of which was spent on shift work (early, late, and nights). I then did five years as a home beat officer on the Isle of Dogs. At the end of that five years, senior management here – that would be the Chief Superintendent, the Superindendent, the Detective Chief Inspector, and the Chief Inspectors – saw that there was a problem with missing people, we were getting so many of them.'

Garrard felt, as many people do, that the missing problem seemed to blow out of proportion in the eighties. In 1989, the year he took the job, there were one thousand three hundred reports of missing persons at his station alone. Before it was his specialism, the report would be received by the crime desk, and someone would be assigned to deal with it. In a routine missing case, a beat officer might go round to sort it out, and in complicated cases, or sinister ones, a CID officer would take it on. 'They were farmed out everywhere,' said Garrard. 'Because we had so many, it was thought – missing persons being very much in the media at that time – it was thought the way forward was to have a dedicated officer.' Garrard's time is taken up, to a large extent, looking for kids who run away from home. They are missing, usually, for no more than a day or two, and sometimes, under good cover, they'll last a bit longer in the care of friends. A bigger problem – at least, one that occurs more often – is that of people going missing from care situations. There are two council-run children's homes in the area, a Barnardo's, and St Clement's Hospital – the psychiatric wing of the Royal London group. Children serially abscond from the homes, and mental patients do the same. Garrard has one boy who went missing over a hundred times in less than a year. He never circulates a missing report until after six hours or so, as many of the missing from care are found and returned within that time.

Most of his longer-term missing are girls. 'It can be a lifestyle thing,' says Garrard. 'I mean, the girls want to be out raving or whatever.' They want a life, I agreed, unlike the one their parents have in mind.

'I had one go missing for six months,' he says. 'She was living in a squat, in Hackney, not a million miles from here. But that was the same problem: broken home, wasn't happy at home, didn't want to go home.' I ask Garrard what happens then, in a situation like that, is there a full-blown inquiry?

'Only sometimes. It's a very fine line we walk,' he says, 'when a kid goes missing, the choice is to pull out all the stops, and cover myself, or use the old sixth sense and say "she'll come back tomorrow".' He knocks on the desk. All the stops, as far as this goes, would include massive publicity – news conferences, local news ads with pictures, a poster campaign, and television appeals – as well as ground searches, house-to-house enquiries, digging, and mass interviews.

Officers like PC Garrard are also responsible for the identification of dead bodies which turn up. He covers the Docklands, and any bodies – suicides or otherwise – discovered at this part of the river or near it become part of his case-load. He tells me he takes all his advice on these cases from PC Clements, the officer at Wapping who is responsible for the identification of bodies found in the Thames. I had already been to see Clements: he was sitting at his desk, scouring pictures, dental records, psychiatric reports, and discharge information, trying to piece together the identity of a woman without a name. He gave her a number; he reckoned she was the sort of woman who would be missed (there were those who were not). I remember thinking, as I spoke to Clements, that he had a very modern job, and that it was one he did with unshakeable concentration.

At Limehouse, Garrard's pager went off mid-sentence. He was telling me about a case of his, one of those he solved, involving a missing son, missed in 1979 by his family, who lived in Hong Kong. The man he was talking about had worked in an overnight hostel for the homeless. After work one evening, he walked out, telling his colleagues he was going to throw himself in the river. This was something he'd said before, and no one paid too much attention. He was never seen again. In 1992, Garrard was sent the missing persons file on this, together with the report – including mortuary photographs – of a body found in the Thames soon after the man's disappearance. The body had remained unidentified. The drowned man must have been without identification when pulled from the water; no one claimed the body at the time, and the connections, for one reason or another, were not made. Garrard was determined to get a result. He wanted to tell the family what had happened to their missing relative, and at the same time put a name to the body of the drowned man, which had been buried by the parish.

He knew, from the photographs in the mortuary file, that the drowned man had some distinctive tattoos on his arm. He went back to the hostel, asking about the man who'd walked out and gone missing in 1979. The manager who was in charge of the place in 1992 had worked there for years, and it had been him who made the initial missing report. He couldn't say, though, when shown the mortuary pictures, if that was his former employee. From old boxes on the premises, they got out hundreds of photographs, and found a picture of someone who the manager thought was the man. Garrard took the picture away, noticing that the figure in the picture was showing a bit of tattoo, and he had it blown up by Photographic. He was sure it was the same man. But it was still a bit iffy – it was hard to tell from both sets of photographs if the tattoo was exactly the same. Garrard went to a tattoo artist and got a positive result. The tattoos weren't English; they'd been done in the Far East. The tattoos were mapped for points, and they came out pretty identical. It was the same man. Garrard went to Hong Kong to tell the family. They were grateful to have a painful mystery finally rubbed from their lives. The coroner re-registered the body from that of an unidentified person to that of the mother's son, the man who'd walked out of his workplace in despair in 1979. His grave is now marked.

'These, unfortunately, are the interesting ones,' said Garrard, leaning back in his chair. 'It's always death that's the interesting subject. That is the way of the world.'

*

MORDEN SOUNDED LIKE what it was: the very last stop on the Northern Line. A young woman with marks on her face had wandered up the platform at King's Cross, trailing a dog on a length of rope. She would stop in front of strangers, her eyes smarting, and ask them for any spare change. I sat on the tube, rattling under central London, and I thought of how each stop going south had less of the city in it, more of the suburb, more of elsewhere. I picked up a bit of a Sunday paper, and read about Cyril Connolly. Brightness came through the window; the train bashed ahead, and the words turned over on the page: 'condemned playground', 'aesthete', 'much promise', '*Horizon*'. By the time the train reached Morden, I was thinking the air might be purer out here. You come out of the tunnel, out of a thickness, and suddenly you arrive in the new world of Surrey.

Mrs Boxell said I should go to the end of the line, then get a bus outside, the number 93, and I should stay on that until it reached the last stop. I knew I was really out of London when I saw a woman being helped onto the bus with her pram; the driver whistled patiently until they were all aboard. I'd forgotten about places like this. Rows of houses and flats would go on for ages, then there would be a clump of shops; then the same houses again, and a quick bite of grocer-Oddbins-videos-hardware-pub. Abbotts Road in Cheam was full of Ford Fiestas and Escorts; most of the houses had those little Tudor beams coming down, and porches, some covered in glass and others twined with green stuff. I used to know a thing or two about birds. As I turned into Mr and Mrs Boxell's close, I spotted – well, you could hardly have missed them – four magpies tumbling over the roofs. It was very quiet; the street was entirely empty.

Pete Boxell had left the front door open – the cat was coming in and out – he may have thought it would help me find them more easily. All the grass was properly cut, and it was nearly good enough to sit outside. Pete shook hands easily, and Christine came through with coffee. The room was full of pictures of their son and daughter. They were a really nice-looking family, very scrubbed and smiley. Pete and Christine were married in 1971. He had been living in Worcester Park before that; she was from Bromley. They moved to this house in 1975, just before their daughter Lindsay was born. Lee was two years old then, and they were one of the first families on the close. They came here for the extra room. In 1980, Pete got a civilian job working for the army in Hanover, and they all moved there, renting this house out while they were gone. Lee and Lindsay went to the British Army school, and they seemed to be very happy. 'It was fantastic,' said Pete, 'those four years. We went on about five holidays a year, all round the Continent. Everything was so close. You know, it was a more exciting life.' Military communities in Germany were always fairly close knit. With so much family, so much routine, left behind in Britain, it was felt by most stationed there that everyone had to club together and make things good. The children had everything, and some thought of it as a sort of perfect childhood. 'I don't suppose they remember it,' said Christine, 'but it was very good.'

Pete's job ended in 1984, and they came back to Cheam. Lee started then at Cheam High School, where he was thought to be a placid, never a brilliant, pupil. He was average. He didn't bunk off; in the regular way, school was just something to be put up with. He didn't like it all that much, but he went, and he did some of the work. He was quite into football, but his coordination wasn't good, and he lacked the confidence to play. He would sometimes kick a ball around just outside the house, or in nearby parks, with his pal Anthony, and he became quite a supporter of Sutton United. He'd often go to their ground. 'He felt safe there,' said Pete. 'He's a sort of shy, modest boy. He was a bit frightened to go to the bigger matches, say, Wimbledon or that. He didn't like to show his colours.'

'Yeh,' said Christine, 'if he did, he'd wear it and hide it.'

He was in the Sutton United supporters' club, and he'd go off with them in the coach to watch away matches. If they were late coming back, he'd always step into a phone box and phone Christine. 'She's a worrier,' said Pete.

'Oh, shush,' she said, giggling.

When he was fifteen, Lee did a few weeks' work experience at Barclays Bank in Cheam. He had a good time, but that's not what he wanted to do. He wanted to become a police officer. 'I had to keep measuring him,' said Christine. He spent whatever money he had on records; he loved pop. First it was Shakin' Stevens, then Whitney Houston, then T'Pau. He stayed in his bedroom a lot, making tapes, listening to records. He never stayed out at night, or stopped over with people: that just wasn't his thing. 'I think he would've liked a girlfriend,' said Christine. 'He once took a girl to a Capital FM roadshow, and he was certainly only interested in girls, but I don't think he knew that many.' Pete handed me some photographs. He did look shy. But like most teenagers, he wore his enthusiasms on the outside. His trainers spoke of an interest in sport, probably football, and his matching jacket and jeans spoke of a careful attitude towards pop music and fashion. He was timid, but not so timid that he couldn't make judgements about what he thought was cool and what wasn't. He was a perfect advertisement for himself, as most teenagers seek to be. His expression was one of growing self-awareness, lurching confidence, and boundless curiosity. Lee was fifteen, and he was right in the middle of his growing up.

It was a hot morning, 10 September 1988. At half-past nine, Pete and Christine were getting ready to go out. Christine was going off to see her mother in Bromley, who wasn't well, and Christine thought to take some things over to her, and then stop the night. Pete was going out shopping, and he said he would drop Lindsay off on the way, at her friend's in North Cheam. Lee was flopped in the chair in his pyjamas, still half asleep, as they were leaving. Pete asked him what he was doing that day, and Lee just mumbled something. They went out of the door. They have never seen Lee again since that morning.

After his family had gone, Lee got dressed and went round the corner for his friend Russell. They walked to Sutton, where they spent the morning going around the shops, looking at records and clothes, and chatting about nothing in particular. They went to McDonald's. Some time after lunch, Lee said he fancied going to see a good match. Russell couldn't go, and he said he was going back home to watch the racing. Russell left Lee in Sutton High Street.

It was the start of the football season and Lee's own team, Sutton United, were playing away in Lancashire. He'd said before that he'd like to go to Selhurst Park, where Millwall were due to play Charlton, and Russell felt that was the game he was headed for. He'd never been to Selhurst Park before, and Pete thinks Lee would've gone to Crystal Palace Station, believing that was near to the ground. He would then have been confused, as the right station for the ground was actually called Selhurst Park, though it was quite a complicated route to work out. Lee was always quite trusting: if someone had got talking to him, and said they'd give him a lift to the match, he would have gone with them. The other possibilities – where he went, how he got there, what happened next – are built from conjecture, and from guesses based on what is known about Lee's character and habits. It seemed very unlikely that he would run away, everyone agrees on that, and it's unlikely he would've got himself disorientated with drugs or drink because he wasn't really interested in that, nor did he know anyone who could get it for him. There are rational explanations: amnesia, accident, misadventure. But none of them really explain the length of time that Lee has been out of sight.

Five years after Lee's disappearance, Christine was having a night out at the local Bingo. She'd been at the loo, and when she came back, her friend said she'd better go over and speak to a woman at a table nearby. 'She's just told me something,' said the friend. Christine went over. The woman, who lived locally and was in Sutton United supporters' club, had seen Lee the day he went missing. He'd been walking up to the railway station in the company of a man.

'Why didn't you tell me before?' Christine said, upset and growing angry.

'My husband,' the woman replied, 'he said I shouldn't get involved.'

The information was passed on to the police, and a description was taken. It turned out that the woman's husband had only recently died, and the woman suddenly felt she could come forward. One officer I spoke to told me things like that happen all the time in missing persons cases. People see something, and they think it's nothing, or they don't think about it, or they don't want to get involved. The details about the movements of missing persons – though they exist: someone must have seen something – are often missing themselves.

On the Saturday afternoon, Pete came back to the house with the shopping. He did some work in the garden, then Lindsay came home, and he made a meal for her. Christine was still in Bromley. Early in the evening, Pete went over the road to see if Lee's friend Anthony was in. There was no one at home, and Pete thought they might have gone to the coast or something, taking Lee along too. Later on, Lee still not back, Pete was talking to Christine on the phone every hour. She was up to high do, beginning to panic, but Pete told her to wait until Anthony's family came back, he'd probably be with them, or maybe he'd gone to a party. All this was very unusual for Lee, but Pete wanted to stay calm. Anthony came back at about 1 a.m., but Lee wasn't with him. Pete started ringing round Lee's friends, and Christine left her mother's in a cab, frantic.

The police came round on the Sunday morning. Christine sat on the sofa, her head full of fear and dread, as they all went out to look for her boy. They went to Sutton High Street, then to parks and football grounds, and eventually to bits of open waste around Cheam. There was no sign. 'We didn't sleep at all,' said Pete, 'we'd just sit up, waiting for a ring at the doorbell, or the telephone. It was like a nightmare.' As he said this to me, Christine stared straight ahead, as if she could see it all plainly right in front of her. 'Every day, you'd think: I'm going to wake up and find he's here and none of this has happened. You'd go to his room and he's not there.' Lee's teachers, and others who knew him, couldn't see any reason why he'd want to run away. He didn't seem troubled, he wasn't in danger. It was a mystery; it was the worst thing imaginable.

'What really got to me,' said Christine, 'was when they went in our loft, when they took his clothes away, and looked in the garage, because it happens, you know, in families. [Murder.] You do wonder, why are they suspecting us, but they have to go by the book. Sadly, it happens.' Superintendent Brendan Gibbs Gray organized a television press conference. One of the investigating officers was a friend of the board of Wimbledon FC, and he persuaded John Fashanu to front the conference. From an incident room in Epsom, a massive search was coordinated. Derelict houses, rivers, railways, parks, malls, housing estates – the whole of suburbia. Then there was the West End. All the time, you'll see homeless juveniles shuffling around central London. Tube stations, river embankments, doorways, amusement arcades, markets, squats, churches, night shelters. People on the streets put the word out to look for Lee. But there was nothing doing; faces turned up that could've been Lee, but they weren't. The police were videoing the crowds at football matches, hoping to see Lee's face among the fans. But nothing.

Teenagers can disappear into the stews of the city, just as adults can, but it was hard to imagine Lee surviving that way of life for long. Most of the kids who do it are fairly hard, or hardened; they're usually big on compulsion, high on volition. That wasn't Lee. Anything like that, any sort of high-risk venture, could only be explained in Lee's case as a non-voluntary thing. He might have been drawn into something against his will. He might have been abducted. As Christmas 1988 came and went, the fearful possibilities began to sink in. Police resources were showing no return, and many had begun to fear the worst. The Boxells kept it up, though. They made thousands of missing posters and sent them to airports, cruise liners, football clubs, race-courses, and one to each of the local shops.

Anyone going on holiday was given one to put up at their hotel. Christine went round the houses with them too, and people would always take one. 'I'd phone up the newspapers,' Christine told me, 'I'd ring them up, and ask them to print something. I remember one of them saying to me, "I'm sorry, Mrs Boxell, but he's just another missing boy." '

I went up to Lee's room, which is still very much as it was. A sky blue quilt covers the bed, and a white desk stands right next to it. The drawers are covered with pop stickers – Queen Live '86; Mel & Kim; Madonna. Many of the posters have fallen down over the years, though there are still a fair few of them up there. In the centre of one wall is a signed picture of Carol Decker, the singer with Lee's favourite group, T'Pau. The *Non-League Club Directory* for 1988 stands on the shelf, next to a coloured-drawing-pins holder in the shape of a light-bulb. Football posters and stickers struggle for space with the pop stuff, and team mugs sit in an even row on the top shelf. His tapes are stacked neatly. Most of them are home-made compilations: things taped off the radio and from the record player. I sat down on the bed with one of his scrapbooks. Lee's writing was neat and curly, clean and self-conscious. On the cover of the book he'd written 'Sutton United Scrap Book. S.U.F.C – Members of the GM Vauxhall Conference Season 88–89. Competitions and Friendlys'. The pages were filled with clippings from the *Sutton Herald*, with Lee's own handwritten commentary down the sides. 'Sutton are experimenting over these friendlys with new signings,' one entry said, 'and reserve players looking a good prospect for the future. Tooting played well against us but we were unlucky not to score. An average match.' I sat a while longer on the blue bed, looking over at his ironed shirts set out on their hangers.

Lee's sister Lindsay is nineteen now. A few years ago, she passed the age Lee was when he disappeared. I was thinking about that. What must it be like to have an older brother frozen like that at a certain age? Your house is full of pictures of him aged fifteen; you remember being younger than that yourself. Your big brother was older than you; and yet you go on and grow past him; he stays where he was, the way you last saw him, just as he's pictured in the frames around you. How mixed up. Maybe in time he'd come to seem like a little brother. Always a little boy, but one who should be, who could be, older than you. Lindsay was studying for exams next door as I sat in Lee's room, studying for exams with her Walkman on. I didn't disturb her then, but I read an article she wrote for the magazine *Just Seventeen*.

'I remember Mum crying and Dad's face going all white with fear,' she wrote, 'then the police arrived in the early hours. I stayed in my room because I couldn't face listening to all the questions they were asking Mum and Dad about Lee and where he liked going.' She goes on: 'Dad spent hours and hours driving around Surrey, searching for him. Then he took Lee's photo up to the West End and began to look in all the places where homeless boys sleep on the streets at night. Mum and Dad have kept his room just as it was on the day he left. I think about Lee every day when I walk past his bedroom. I miss him so much.' It wasn't a big room, Lee's; it was one of those box rooms every boy knows; one of those little places where everything happened, where records or books or teams or girls or whatever, happened – where all of it filled your head, every other night, under a sixty-watt bulb.

Lee is nowhere to be seen. A man came by one time, saying he saw Lee Boxell working on a market stall in Brixton. Pete went there, and he couldn't believe his eyes. 'He was the double of Lee,' Pete said. 'I had to speak to him. After a few years, you know, you begin to think you might have forgotten what your son looked like. You begin to think he might have looked a bit more like that. This boy was so like him. His voice was different, though. I was beginning to think maybe I should ask him to come and live with us; he was so like him. Just come here and be our son. You get these ideas, you know. But it wasn't him.'

'It's worse than knowing he's dead. It really is. This way, we'll never give up trying to find him; we'll keep going till we know what happened.' Christine went out to collect some washing off the rope. 'Sometimes I think he's alive somewhere,' Pete said, 'and other days I think he's dead. You know the way you can go up and down?' I think that I do. When Christine came back, I said goodbye to them, and they waved me away at the door. On my way down Abbotts Road, past all these pretty houses, I felt miles away from everything. High-flying RAF planes, the ones that cut a white line across the sky, were crisscrossing up above. I hadn't seen that in years. I really hadn't seen it in years.

PEOPLE GET LOST, their life-stories disappear, and the lingering detail is all we know of them. The police take charge of the information, and it's their business to compare it with information about others. The flow of data between police divisions and New Scotland Yard has been thought by many to be ineffective, so far as missing persons is concerned. The more that was collected, the less observed. Information was thought to be piling up, and obscuring itself. Cross-referencing and selection wasn't easy; it wasn't working well. The computer held on to cases that had been reported missing but were later found: but the finding wasn't noted. It also kept word of some cases occurring outside of London, but not all these by any means. In 1979, the Council of Europe was considering police practices and looking at procedures on missing persons. It was felt that there should be national offices which would act as clearing houses for all the information on people who'd been missing for more than twenty-eight days. It also envisaged a network of information that would prove useful at an international level. 'The tracing of missing persons', stated one council document, 'is very much a humanitarian problem of great importance not only to the individual and the family but also to society and the state. No one can remain unmoved by the mental, physical or economic distress that may be experienced by the missing person, or the anxiety, emotional loss and difficulties suffered by the family.'

In 1994, following much debate, a response to this came with the establishment, in London, of the National Missing Persons Bureau. This unit is still finding its feet, and will probably, in time, provide the basis for a British National Identification System. Its function is broad, and unsure. It does not organize searches; it doesn't have any counselling function; it is not a publicity machine. Its role has mainly to do with 'matching'. It stores information on missing individuals, and data on unidentified bodies, and tries to establish links between them, as well as identifying patterns that may prove crucial in a murder inquiry. The new computer came too late for eleven missing girls in Gloucester – who were everywhere in the news the day I walked passed the eternal flame at the door of Scotland Yard – but its £250,000 brain will doubtless aid future inquiries of that sort. People missing from Glasgow, say, in 1968, might be found to have resided at an address in Gloucester, an address associated with the names of other people, from other places, who are also known to be missing.

The rooms containing the national bureau are full of clean terminals, all of them connected to the new database. The walls are covered with faces, some of them lively and smiling, and others obviously dead. Jackie, a soft-spoken officer in plain clothes, tells me how it works. She hands me a typical printout, one with the misper's name left off. The information is set out in columns and in boxes; it is a standard form, containing fine detail that will be stored for cross-checking. The missing person I'm reading about was born on New Year's Day, 1934. She was sixty years old when she went missing. The information was passed to the bureau by Essex Police, at South Ockendon police station. My eye traipsed down the columns:

HEIGHT:	504		
BUILD:	Medium	COMP:	Fair
HAIRC:	Lt Brown	COAT:	Jacket
HAIRD:	Curly	UOUTR	Jumper Green
HAIRL:	Shoulderl	UINNR:	Shirt Green
EYESC:	Brown	LOWER:	Trousers Black
EYEGL:		FEET:	Shoes Black
HFACE:		OTHER:	

As I look over this, I form an idea of the missing woman. The boxes tell me she was wearing a chain; she has an abdominal scar; she has a tattoo on her arm; she takes tablets for some unspecified illness. Below that, there is some general stuff, under a heading FREE TEXT. She went missing from 123 High Street;

she was seen by someone in the evening; it is thought she may have gone out to get her pension. She failed to return; suffers from Alzheimer's. I'm told she is an example – there may be no such woman missing, and there may be many such as this. You could call up a list of all the missing women in Britain, aged sixty, with an abdominal scar. The database whirs quietly, and the list comes up on screen. It will give the names of those twenty-four years below the specified age, and fifteen years above. As often as not, a little message will blink up, saying *no trace*.

Clive Marriot works next door, at the Metropolitan Police Missing Persons Bureau. This department has been on the go since 1929. It was long thought to perform the role of a national bureau, but it was really only meant for those missing in London. Divisions of the Metropolitan Police – like Chris Garrard's branch at Limehouse – send in a teleprinter message for all their mispers cases still missing six hours after the initial report comes in. Other forces in Britain, if they have reason to believe the misper may have headed for the Met area, would notify the bureau, though ownership of the case always resides with the local station. Marriot outlined some of the difficulties. They weren't there to initiate national searches off their own bat. They felt themselves to be more of a clearing house for information than anything else; they had current records going back to 1961, and these were computerized. They would now and then search their records at the request of a family, looking to find a name or a body to match the information given. Marriot said they did this as a PR exercise; they weren't a family tracing service, and most of their work was in relation to those who may have come to some harm. They aren't social workers: they have an interest in making successful matches, and in apprehending criminals. Many missings will turn out to involve some sort of crime, it seems. The missing person may just have slipped out of sight on purpose, knowing the advantage of not being identified. At the very least, most missing cases constitute, in one way or another, a set of very suspicious circumstances. The computers may lead them to sites of foul play – to victims, to connections between victims, and to the establishment of a victim's name. It may also, in the end, lead to the names of certain sorts of perpetrators.

Other officers will say – though never on record – that police work being done on missing persons may prove to be a testing ground for the larger ambitions of national identification. If the essence of everyone's documentary lives can be got on a national computer, some say, then the detection of fraud, of theft, of hooliganism, of abduction, and of serial murder, will become a matter of computer elimination, of 'matching', aided by the usual police procedures. The missing problem can be complexly evil, and it can be complexly benign. It may in time be answered by a national system of watching which helps with the stamping out of all sorts of badness, but which also prevents people who want to lose themselves from doing so. This, perhaps, is the price to pay. It may turn out to be a necessary price, though not at all an insignificant one. It pays for a very modern sort of watchfulness. A decent and effective welfare state was once thought to be the admirable thing, an institution able to drive a nation's watching over itself, but maybe that is now quite out of style. 'Things have gone a certain way,' said one care worker I spoke to, who looks for stray juveniles on London's streets, 'and there's reasons for the increase in numbers of missing persons. People are more desperate, and there's less for them, less help. Some of those missing, some of them are just *out* there with nothing securing them down.'

IT WAS ALREADY dark, and everything was wet. The old woman had tea. She motioned to me, and I went over beside her. We were in the Strand, where she often slept, and she just wanted to talk a minute. She seemed like she might be suffering from Alzheimer's, or maybe from amnesia. I didn't know enough about either – or about her – to tell. But she spoke fast, though not all of it made sense. She thought she was Dolly. When I asked her where she'd lived before she said she thought Stratford or something. Maybe she had sons, four sons, but she couldn't right remember. I asked the guy in the van, the terse captain of the soup kitchen, if he could give me more tea for her. She was sort of laughing and chattering to nowhere. I asked if people knew where she was. She sniggered, and blew into the tea. 'Nobody knows nothing,' she said.

Just off Shaftesbury Avenue, at the beginning of Dean Street, there's a place called 'Centrepoint: Off the Streets'. It's not meant for homeless like Dolly (there's other places, emergency night shelters, filled with the old). This one's for young people in the West End, who do their thing around the streets there, and who might want to be indoors now and then. The main room has sofas and bookshelves, and baskets of plums. There are heaps of magazines, scatter cushions, and blue table-tops ready to eat off. The London hostels meant for older vagrants – such as Camden Nightshelter, and Bondway in Vauxhall – are basic and dank; they do the job, but are quite grim. Centrepoint is the opposite of that. It's clear that they want to appear more optimistic; the place itself looks stylish and young, clean and hopeful. Radios are playing, board-games are there, and the food is good and hot. A bellyful of laundry was tumbling in the drier as I walked around downstairs. There were separate dormitories for men and women, and everything was scrubbed. Over a bed at the women's end was a coloured advertising poster, announcing the publication of a new Peter Ackroyd novel. It's like an idea of home, a sort of floating homeliness, which (according to the rules) can be enjoyed no more than eight days a month by a homeless youngster.

Those who pass through those rooms are unknown. They will be asked for a first name, an age, and where they come from, but no one who gives a true answer to these small questions is giving anything away. They remain in almost every sense anonymous. They may come only once, they may appear quite regularly and then never again, they may seem always to be somewhere near, they might come and never want to leave. But they keep most of themselves to themselves, and don't get involved in explanations or consequences or follow-throughs. They're secret. That's not to say they won't speak – they will, about most things – but they won't give themselves up, or away, and won't allow details to go from them which are likely to prove useful in the keeping of tabs. Many are decisively lost, always for running away. They just wander, and escape, and keep running, and stay out of it. For some, this is a tacit agreement between them and their sometime guardians. Being a family doesn't suit either side, so they all blow. Sometimes the family changes, or changes its mind, and decides to make a go of it, but often little Racine is gone, and there's to be no finding her then. A lot of the kids I spoke to had no sense of their relatives' worries: they mostly thought people were glad to be rid of them. Some knew themselves to be missing, though most reckoned they'd never been reported as such. Little Racine, the nineteen-year-old mother in the blue Kangol hat, wasn't sure 'they' knew who she was now, but she was still sure about 'them': they were no good; they'd all hurt her; none of them had any right to know of her existence, much less to follow it.

Racine told me she knew loads of young people in her position. She said the streets were full up. She rolled her eyes when I asked her about those pictures of missing people in the *Big Issue*. 'This woman, right, she came up to me. And I'm like, no way, I can't deal with this. She shows me a picture of this missing girl, who's like my friend and that, and she was upset, looking for her daughter, but I just couldn't say anything. I couldn't give her away.' Racine has been missing herself, though she recently phoned some old foster parents to tell them she was fine. She was living on the streets while she was pregnant; sitting, she told me, on the steps of Top Shop in Oxford Street, crying, and waiting for something to happen. I asked her what happened then. She took another cigarette.

'What happened?'

'Where did you go to then?'

'I was here, in here, when the waters broke.'

'Here. When was that?'

She twisted the fag from the corner of her mouth, and sniffed. 'Two weeks ago.'

Racine's child was being looked after by Social Services; but she wanted to give it a proper home herself. 'If I could just have a house,' she said, 'and could make it work.'

Pete McGinlay, who runs the project in Dean Street, is a big man with a grizzly beard. He has a nice touch; he is very obviously sympathetic, and careful. He is quick to spot tension or rambling in the young people who come in – including the journalists who come in – and he will bring down the volume, easing things, taking the piss, and just being a bit human and sorting out people's anxieties. You get the impression he may have had a few of his own, but he seems to let the experience, rather than the words, do the talking. He's the opposite of patronizing, the reverse of a boss-pleaser, and he has a fine sense of social history, a soft spot for society, that is all the more engaging for not being dogmatic or at all hectoring. We sat in the afternoon, with giant mugs of tea.

'A lot of the people we see here,' he says, 'haven't got a home to go to. Many are from care, and there's no going back there. The local authority, which is perhaps the biggest mother of them all, says you must go when you are sixteen, and many of them do.' He feels strongly about confidentiality. The Dean Street operation was set up in 1990 under funding rules which differed from the usual ones. Other hostels would ask for information such as your National Insurance number and the like, so that they could make a claim for rent, reimbursement for having put the individual up. The Housing Benefit Office would accept claims only if accompanied by proper identification, such as NI numbers. There is no obligation to give such information at Centrepoint.

'Where do they go from here,' I ask him, 'where abouts?'

'About forty-two per cent of those who leave here will say they're leaving to go into longer-term accommodation – that could be into a long-term hostel, or a bedsit or flat scheme. They can tell me that, and I can mark it down as a statistic, but nothing will tell me they stayed there the night after telling me. Some will be back again, because the tenancy will not have worked. But, really, I don't have the right to know what people do when they've moved on. I don't really want to know. What you do know is that a large number of those who come here over the years disappear; they're disappearing, and the best thing you can do to maintain your own sanity is to assume that they're doing OK. You can't bear to imagine them out there, in hell, in worse circumstances than what they were in the last time you saw them.'

Centrepoint opened in 1969, and was accommodating young people under thirty, but over the years, the average age has gone down and down. There used to be more young people on the streets of London than anywhere else. But now, in the nineties, there is an increasing number who are homeless in, say, the North, who are responding to homeless projects in their own area. It wasn't really possible, before, to be homeless in Liverpool and Glasgow and to have a life spent between day centres and night shelters.

There were vagrants and winos, for sure, but there was no network for young homeless. They would go to London, and be on the streets there, where more and more young people situated themselves, and where many organizations formed around that situation. These days, there is a young homeless problem in every big space in Britain: Oxford has it, and so does Dundee; Birmingham, Cardiff and Gloucester have it too. And there are agencies now, people responding to this explosion in the numbers of youngsters who are homeless in the vicinity of their former homes.

'It's one thing to leave your housing estate and head for Glasgow city centre,' said McGinlay, 'but if you make the bigger jump and go all the way to London, you might just never make it back. You might not. So we had to look towards funding provision in the local areas.'

Pete McGinlay had gone from Glasgow to London, and so

had I, and it was true that no one ever went back to Glasgow saying London was crap. It was always brilliant, even when it was not. There was a tradition in Glasgow – as elsewhere, dwindling now – of people jumping on the bus to London and never coming back. There was a sub-tradition, too, of people, the majority of people, who did come back and who talked about London, and how good it had been, for the rest of their lives. There was always London, just as there was always New York. My cousin Stevie came to London, to King's Cross as it turned out, and he never gave his parents an address. Stevie was a character, and London offered him some kind of promise, though the promise was always a secret. He'd be away for months and months, without a word. Then he'd phone – from the Bell, or the Pilton, or the Flying Scotsman – and sing down the phone to his mum. That was it, and that was how it was always described. Stevie had his own life, and he'd a good family behind him, but they *were* behind him, he was always a step ahead. In the late eighties, Stevie was found in a coma, lying at the bottom of some concrete steps in his adopted city. London, the big smoke, or something, had got to him. People talked of a fall, but Stevie looked as if he'd had his lights kicked in. He died at Glasgow's Royal Infirmary one night, soon after he'd been brought there, and no one had much to say. It was unthinkable. After the funeral mass at St Paul's on Shettleston Road, and a summary cremation, a relative stood with me in the Gartoka Bar, talking about how blessed a footballer young Stephen had been. People always talked about Stevie as if they were talking about the seventies. Then he was something else: brilliant, all promise, but growing more discontented by the day. 'If he'd stayed here,' said the relative, 'and stayed away from *that*' – pointing to a pint – 'he'd've been a star striker.'

No one could believe Stevie was gone. The world seemed all of a sudden poor, our cities rotten in the middle, and everything to do with his snuffing out looked cold and confusing and remote. London was to blame.

McGinlay ran his hand over his beard, and tapped on the table with a pen. 'A man came here taking pictures once,' he said. 'I had him downstairs, and one of the pictures was of me giving a young guy pillowcases or something. The guy's face was defibrillated, pixilated, whatever you call it – obscured in the photograph – and the following week, after it was published in a newspaper, we got a letter and a new jumper addressed to the guy, from his mother. She'd recognized the jumper he was wearing in the photograph. There was nothing in the article to give him away – false name, different town, but they saw it, they looked at it, and thought, "It's my boy," 'cause they wanted to see that.'

There's a missing persons file in the office here, and McGinlay will tell visiting young mispers that someone is looking for them, and he might suggest that they phone. He thinks it's not right, though, it's sort of beyond his power, to phone parents or relatives himself. He won't do that. 'Even if you know somebody's mother is breaking her heart over it, you can't get involved. You don't have the right. The kids have the right to have a good reason for it not to be known they are here. You'll talk to people on the phone, distressed beyond words, who can't find another way of asking, "Have you seen him?", "What does he look like?"; they think you're keeping something back; these people don't think he's in London making £12,000 a week and playing for Arsenal; he's hiding in London 'cause he'd *got* something.'

I nod, then say that some would expect people in his position to catch these youngsters. 'We can only do what we do,' McGinlay says. 'We give them a bed for the night, breakfast in the morning, and the opportunity to come back tomorrow night. That's a sort of frame, if you like, and they can try to solve the other things within that.' The tea was freezing now, the light was going, and I was running out of tape. The place was quiet, and I wanted to ask something else.

'Would you say you'd always been political?'

'I had this dream of being a Communist,' he said. 'I ended up with the Militant bit of the Labour Party for five years: I'd found a better way of wasting my time.'

We talked about work and family, and I asked him if politics led him to this sort of thing. 'No,' he said, unfurling a grin. 'Not at all. I'm not here looking for therapy.'

A week later, at another table, I sat between a boy called Sammy and a girl, Angel. The boy's talk was all over the place; his eyes were pale, with pupils like pin-heads. He was speeding (someone on the street, he told me, had given him some cocaine-and-speed thing to smoke), and he couldn't shut up. He kept thanking everybody, telling them his name, asking question after question, and rolling out commentary on everything. He'd suffer little bursts of paranoia, where he thought everybody at the table was laughing at him, but he was fine. He just kept talking. Angel was making her way through a giant plate of spaghetti. Her face was pretty close to the plate, and she was chewing away, with eyes looking up at Sammy's antics. She had one of the most unusual faces I've ever seen. One minute, it would be serene, and open, and quite beautiful, and the next it would go hard and very aggressive. Just like that. She had her first face on when talking about pop music or women she'd meet outside, and her second face would clunk into place when she started talking about boys.

I went to another part of the building with Angel. I put all the cigarettes on the table, and she smoked away, lighting one off the other. She told me she's obsessed with an Irish boy called Mikey. He supports Chelsea; she would call a baby Chelsea. Her wrists were covered with scratches, slashes, and she'd bruises, home-made tattoo scars, and burn marks on different parts of her neck and arms and legs. She sees Mikey around the streets, and in places like this sometimes, and he's always with a gang. They're all homeless.

Angel was born in 1974, in Hammersmith. Her mother abused her when she was two – one time she had fifty-four bruises on her body – and left her when she was very young. Her father was away before her mum left, but then he came back, and he looked after her with his new wife. 'He built the TV aerial up on Fortune Green,' she said. 'Every time I walk past that aerial I think of him.'

Angel talks about violence as if completely in awe of it. She talks of a killing she was involved in at King's Cross, halfway up Caledonian Road, where she carved her name on the victim's body. I don't know if it happened, and I don't want to know, but she said the girl was dead, and now they've 'made up spiritually'. She sniffed and drew tight on her fag. 'She knows now why I did it,' she said. She tells me she was put in a detention centre in Reading and then in Holloway Prison, but her dates don't tally with her age. I stop asking questions for a while, and just let her ramble. When she talks about pop groups, she smiles and raptures, but then she links her liking for them to some horrendous physical abuse or violent episode. 'When I was into New Kids on the Block,' she says, 'everyone treated me like a cunt. I was into NKOB when I was seventeen, right, and I saw girls getting raped, attacked, beaten up. I got battered. Now that I'm into East 17 everything has just rolled like a smooth train. New Kids are bastards. East 17 are sweet as ... I heard Wet, Wet, Wet's new song, and I just picked up the blade, put it in Indian ink, and went smash, smash.' She points to her wrist, and shows me her new tattoos, still raw and bloody. She sleeps around Euston and Vauxhall, and isn't allowed into many of the night shelters because she won't produce identification.

Angel is not being looked for any more. No one is trying to find her now, and the last thing she wants is to be found. She ends up, sometimes, in rooms with groups of men, and she takes her clothes off. She does it because they ask her to. She told me that Mikey, the one she's in love with, would just use her for sex and a punch-bag. I ask her why she's attracted to him when she knows he's like that. She blows her lips out, and shrugs. 'Because I'm like that.' She came into the West End because she thought it would be getting away, jumping into the world. She now has large red weals around her neck, where someone had tried to strangle her. She's beyond everything. That's what she tells me. When she was younger, she was seeing social workers and psychiatrists for being obsessed with New Kids on the Block. I watch her for ages; her eyes are closed, she sings to herself, a cigarette between her fingers. Outside, you could hear Soho bump and grind; lights flashed through the window at us, and a bunch of late-night Soho good-timers rolled past. Smoke curled upwards. 'Angel, what do you want to happen?' I asked.

'Only one thing,' she said. 'I want to sing at Wembley Stadium, wearing a gold top and a black skirt. I want to hear thousands and thousands of applause.'

AT THE HEAD of his Salvationists in 1885, William Booth

worried about missing persons, about those he preferred to call 'the lost' or 'the fallen'. London was a black hole, as all big cities increasingly were, and girls poured out of the shires, out of the counties, heading for a chosen city, many of them hopeful of a place downstairs in one of the grand houses. London was full of lighted shops, carriages, long banisters, and promise, and young people were drawn to it then, as they have been since. Needless to say, many of them didn't make it. They'd make it to London well enough, but then get waylaid on the way to the grand houses. And many who secured a position would leave it, would find the work hard and the life dark, and would just disappear into the city drink.

In the issue of the *War Cry* for 11 July 1885, Booth addressed this, and announced a half-dozen proposals to be taken up by the Salvation Army: '1. Any forsaken, helpless, friendless girl can come for counsel and assistance at any hour; 2. Any white slaves can run from their prison houses and can be assisted; 3. Foreign girls unable to speak English can come for advice and assistance; 4. Girls can write when detained in houses against their will; 5. Girls who have not entirely made up their minds to abandon the life can be talked to and prayed with; 6. Parents who have lost a girl can apply for information.'

The first missing notices went up around London within weeks. *Missing. Margaret Jarrard, eighteen years of age, fair complexion, short and very stout. Father and mother will receive her gladly. Address: 4 Eliza Place, Walker Street, Hull.* Mrs Booth's Enquiry Office, as it was known for a time, quickly attracted thousands of missing person enquiries. Mr Booth was pleased, but typically unsatisfied. He wanted more society, he yearned for ripened community, and the saving of souls. He wanted to populate heaven from the accidental denizens of hell.

There was much to be done in William Booth's *Darkest England*, much Victorian complacency to break through. Booth lived – mindful of poverty, loss, and vice – at the blinking-out of a late-nineties Britain. He lived fifty years before the welfare state came to make things better.

These days, the Salvation Army traces relatives through its international network of members and offices. It has two offices in London devoted to this work. The Army's searches put the emphasis on reunion. That's the point, for them: bringing estranged families and partners together, or finding whether a lost or gone individual is alive or dead, freeing the abandoned spouse to remarry, or whatever. They will seldom be involved in mispers cases where foul play is suspected; they will not bring unwilling husbands back, or force mothers to face daughters they once sent out for adoption. But they will forward letters to people living somewhere, even ones with a new identity, if there's good reason to do so. (The DSS will do this too, if the circumstances are right, and, of course, if they have a record of the missing addressee.)

Other Salvationists, a great number of whom are still involved in street work, will encourage young mispers and other vagrants to let an officer phone home, or pass on a message. But they are discreet, and they are careful. They are also tied, as it were, to universal problems, not those of Britain alone, or even this world now. The Salvation Army have always been slightly out of it. They want to do positive things, and do them in the way they always have. They don't see beyond that, and that's fine with them, and it should be sort of all right with us too. After all, the present grime, the detail of today's troubles, is not what ultimately matters to them. 'Jesus was a missing person,' wrote one investigator. 'As a boy of twelve, on his first visit to Jerusalem, he was lost to his parents for three days. The Salvationist who is engaged in tracing people is not astonished to find the ever-present Christ in seemingly unlikely situations.'

THE OFFICE OF the National Missing Persons Helpline is one large room – fluorescent, and noisy with ringing phones – and it sits on top of a supermarket in Upper Richmond Road West. The people at the desks are searching, publicizing, counselling, cross-referencing, matching, and very often finding the people who go with the names, the details, that they have gathered and stored. They are detectives and social workers, worldly campaigners, and their role has become central, their expertise and concentration something new. It started off around 1990 with one mobile phone.

Publicity was very early thought to be the big weapon. Television especially. They now have various slots in the morning, a regular evening slot on Carlton, and an hour-long programme called *Missing*. These broadcasts work well, so far as finding people goes. They seem to be watched, and the audience are able to ring the freephone numbers which are flashed up for them. There's a rising awareness: people go missing, people might find them. There's always a downside, though, and the one with television is that – whatever else, whatever social purpose it abets – television must be entertainment first and foremost. Many of the missing stories are therefore done in the tabloid fashion – with hammed-up reconstructions, chilling music, tremulous narration, and no opportunity lost for a murder-mystery cliché. On the other hand, the helpline has a national audience, and that's the one thing mispers have never had in a regular way before.

Mary Asprey, one of the founders, always looks busy, almost too busy to stop. She sat next to me, but every now and then she'd be up and off, taking calls and sorting things. Her voice is stridently polite, and she's all for the facts; she won't waste time, though she might fritter a little away with someone who's writing a book, if only to save him from making the obvious mistakes. She's cynical, but gives every impression of having her reasons for that. Before meeting her, I felt that the worlds of the missing – places where many of my concerns had gathered, dispersed, and oddly returned – were more interesting to me than to most anyone else. But I could see that Mary was more taken up with it than I was. I could see that she was more rational about it too. It may have been personal to her, but just as likely it was not. She kept her head above it, and was more interested in the practicalities. For her, things might have meanings, but they might just as well not. People went missing. It meant nothing, really. It wasn't about meaning: there were causes and there were certain effects. She was all for the facts: each person was missing because of something; most could be recovered if the case were handled effectively. I sat taking notes. Yes, some of the cases were inexplicable. Bodies were hidden, accidents happened, abductions took place, new lives were got, kids might be swallowed up in the city. Who knows? And so what? There are things to be done about it.

I kept on listening. Mary was right, there were things that could be done, and she was one of the ones doing them. The charity was a success, it really did answer to a lot. I knew that, from the people they'd served. I was always being told as much, by mispers' families, by recovered mispers themselves. The Helpline was doing the main job. In their practical way they cared about these missing lives; Mary and her colleagues were on to them; they were helping the survivors; and recovering some of the people lost. I looked at her, and took more notes. I knew that Mary was right, but I also knew that her account wasn't wholly right for me. It was correct, but it wasn't all there was to say. It wasn't the end of the story. Modern life is full of traumatized bystanders; the aches and pains of the nearly involved. Sometimes, we might know what went on, have an idea of what occurred, and yet we know nothing about it, except that we are changed now, and we must accept that we can be changed by things we don't understand. Kids had been snatched off the street, whilst other kids played around them, and adults went on their way. Those who notice the missing will say, now and then, that nothing could ever be the same again. And neither it could, not for anyone.

A SCHUBERT CD played at the other side of the room. You would have to say that the coroner seemed a bit wild, as he whistled and flailed in the cupboard, conducting the music whilst he waited for the kettle. His office hid at the end of a very white corridor somewhere in the Barbican, and I sat there, again, waiting for news on the missing and the dead. It might sound obvious, but one of the things you notice about the coroner classes is how cheerful they are. They're always laughing. Ten months before this morning's meeting with Dr Chambers, I'd been at the mortuary in Camley Street, near St Pancras, talking to the statistician. He was talking about London's unknown dead, giving me the figures and talking about his work, and he'd break off now and then to tell a joke. They do that, and you guess it's their way of handling it or something. The stats man was on about sudden death – where someone dies alone, in their house, and nobody notices for ages – and he'd break off to say something humorous about the ways of old people. Dr Chambers was the same: always ready to see the funny side of the dark side.

His office was somewhere to rest awhile. Everything was so nicely arranged you felt you might just stay put; you might eat off the table, snooze on the chairs, and brush your teeth or comb your hair at the little sink just through the back. And Dr Chambers himself was entirely at home, as befits such a place, and rightly at home with himself. He left the music on as we spoke, nodding at me as he put down the tea. 'There,' he said, though he might have said it twice, he might have said, 'There, there.' Chambers was an expert on death. He made it his business to establish causes of death, and dealt with registering the names of dead people, and thinking what to do when their identity was unknown. Identity unknown. The words swayed a little, out in front, as he talked on. He would chuckle now and then. The tea was all milk. You can't see what's alive till you can know what's dead; you can't know society till you've known history; you can't see the present till you've opened up the past. You'll find what is here, something of how we live here, if you can only see what has gone now, what has gone from here, what has left us behind. He seemed to say all of this, and none of it, as the morning went away, and the shade took over.

'Death is a less frequently occurring thing,' he said. And he said a lot of things like that, in exact little sentences, measuring out his forty years' experience in level spoonfuls. He meant there was less disease, less death by natural causes, but I thought he meant more than that. I thought he was saying that we were less sure of death; we didn't notice it the same way. I said that Britain had such a problem with missing persons, and many of them weren't known to be dead or alive. Most would be alive, somewhere, I guessed. But many wouldn't be. There is no less murdering than there used to be, but there are fewer bodies to show for it. Dr Chambers rocked a little, and used his hands as he spoke. He told me how things used to be. 'When I was first doing this job, if someone – one of these sudden death cases as we call them now – died alone, and their body lay there for months, or even years as it sometimes is, then it would be something of a scandal. It would be a story in the *Daily Telegraph*. Everyone would say, "How can this happen?", "Why wasn't she missed?", "What's going on?" There was a great deal of concern. But now, yes, now I see many cases of that sort. They're just gone, and no one notices. Many of them, many people who go like that, have outgrown everyone. There may be no one left alive who knows who they are.' The local authorities will sometimes have large inquiries, but they go past, like the dead that occasioned them, largely unnoticed by the world.

Dr Chambers was born in Camden Town, and practised for most of his professional life in that part of London. He talked about his mother a lot, and drew many comparisons between them. 'If there was someone living alone,' he said, 'then my mother would keep an eye out. If the person's curtains weren't open two mornings in a row, over she'd be, over the fence, to see what was wrong.' But he's pretty open minded about it. Maybe people care just as much nowadays; maybe they move around more; or perhaps people just have too much to do. 'It's not anybody's fault, not any one person. Maybe things will go the other way again.' The coroner has daughters and a son, and they've had their ups and downs. He joked about it all, about family and the future, and told me how things usually work out all right in the end. We walked together through the corridors of the Barbican, winding down to the road, and we continued towards Liverpool Street Station, where he caught the train. Before he went off, I said I wanted to ask him one more thing. 'The work,' I said, 'does it get to you sometimes?'

'It doesn't do,' he said. 'What with my girls' interesting matrimonial careers and such like, I've got enough to be dealing with. Everyone has their own tragedies to bear, you know?' He tapped on my arm and smiled, and disappeared into a funnel of people.

Dr Chambers' thing about the *Daily Telegraph* stuck in my mind. It would just come into my head now and then, as I was out drinking, or posting letters, or picking up laundry. It wasn't bothering me or anything, it was just there, inside, and I knew about it. It was just a little bit of lingering detail – a sliver of information encoding change – lodged in amongst the other things that might come up in a day. There had been an increase in the number of people in Britain who might die on their own, and lie undiscovered. It was a thing now. To be missing before, you would have to have been lost and come to harm, or taken yourself away to a new and anonymous life, or have been abducted or seduced into something ill-apparent, or perhaps you'd be murdered and hidden, or maybe you'd lost your mind, or your memory, and gone all the way out of reach. You might have run away, to be far from harm; or maybe you had run towards some idea of glamour, where new harm lay waiting. These were some of the things I'd found, and some of the missing I'd got to, during my searches. But this thing of Dr Chambers' was something else. People might go very undramatically, very quietly, and be there in their community all the while. They may go missing, in fact, but never be thought of that way. They may just live next door, as they always had, but be dead, and dead to the world.

The Public Health Act, 1984 updated the National Assistance Act of 1948. Section 50 of the original Act (now called Section 46, following the order of the most recent legislation) made it a statutory requirement of local authorities to arrange the funerals of persons found dead in their catchment area. The 1948 Act replaced and improved the Poor Law of 1840, and attempted, among other things, to give order and dignity to the affair still known as a parish funeral. The pauper's grave, or public grave, is still used, and the costs will be defrayed – in circumstances where there is no money, or no family to take over – by the local council.

People who die without family or friends will often lie undiscovered for some time, and many will be found by accident. Most will become coroner's cases for a period, and that period can go from a few days to several months depending on the circumstances. Council officers, under the direction of the coroner, will first have to establish the person's name, for death registration is the first priority. Cause of death will then be ascertained, though if a person has lain too long it is not an easy, or sometimes even a possible, thing to establish. Finally, there is the business of the funeral. Local authorities employ someone (sometimes several someones) to arrange funerals, and the payment of them. It is part of their job to visit the house of the deceased, to go through what's there, to confirm the identity of the dead person, and to find out the names of possible relatives and friends. It's one of those modern jobs that needs doing, and those I spoke to who do it were sensitive and careful and stoic in the face of such pitiful circumstances.

The documentary lives of many who live, and die, in solitude will often be hidden under dust. The details will seem lost, even to their closest neighbours and to family living another life – perhaps even to the person himself – and it will need to be rebuilt. Many older folk who live in local authority housing have their rent paid by direct debit, or by the DSS directly, so there is no need for visits or paperwork after the initial signing, which in any case may have been decades before. Martin, one of the funeral officers I spoke to, said many people in that situation were out of touch with NI numbers, tax stuff, medical records, and all the other paperwork that coats the visible body. They may have a pension, but that's all. Some pensions go unclaimed for years. They might make a regular but fairly anonymous journey to the supermarket and back. And that might be it. Martin said when he goes into a house he'll sit there, going through piles of letters, usually old letters, and reading diaries, shopping lists, old apprenticeship papers, college certificates, trying to piece things together. It's a weird thing, that, he says, building up lives from bits of paper, from scraps and belongings that are left behind. Some of them led ever such interesting lives at one time.

They'll also be looking for evidence of an estate, though mostly, with people who die like that, there isn't one. If there is, the money will go towards a better funeral than the local authority could afford, and it will go to the family if they can be found. If no one turns up, it will go to the Treasury. Martin says it's worth doing anything you can to find someone, preferably a relative. The last time I spoke to him he was working on a case where a man had died alone in North London. He found a number in an old diary belonging to the man, the number of a woman. She'd moved away, and he had to keep ringing directory enquiries, and sending off letters to dubious names, till he reached the woman whose name it was. She used to be married to the man's brother; her husband died six years before, but she still had the number of one of the sisters. The sister lived in County Durham, and Martin went up there on the train. It seemed to be the right connection, though she hadn't set eyes on the man for thirty-one years. Martin sent her all the photographs, personal papers and the man's Masonic medals, and is waiting to hear. If the woman in Durham can't pay for the funeral that's OK, the funeral officer will explain that they can provide a basic service. Most people are sad and surprised to learn that such and such is dead. They might have forgotten them a bit, or thought they were dead already, or abroad, but most say they'd no idea of the circumstances.

Where there's no family or friends, or much in the way of paperwork, old diaries, or photographs, the funeral person may have to guess a bit. If they have a name, that's fine, but if they don't have any evidence of religion then they might have to take a chance. A standard Church of England service usually does it – always burial, not cremation, just in case they later turn out to have been a Catholic. If the officers have anything to go on, they will arrange things to suit the deceased. Martin's department has done Muslim services, Hindu, Buddhist, Baptist, Methodist, C. of E., Catholic, Seventh-Day Adventist. 'The lot,' he says. There have been cases recently where not even the name of the dead person was known. There were four in a row, all of whom died in small hotels in central London, all of whom were registered under false names. Most of them died of drug overdoses, and they had nothing on them, not a thing. When the names they'd given were checked – for National Insurance, medical registration, DSS claims – they all turned up a 'no trace' signal. They were all buried by the local authority, their graves marked *Unknown Male*, or *Unknown Female*. That was the end of it.

A twenty-year-old man lay dead in his flat in Camden. The flat was in a dreadful state. He had been living on his own. There was nothing there, besides him. He was on housing benefit. It looked like he might have come from Manchester, but it was hard to find a match for him among the list of Manchester's reported missing persons. There were no belongings, no papers, and he didn't even look like himself any more. The flat was grim. A few chairs, a kingdom of bugs, the floor thick with dirt and stale things. The boy had lain dead for six weeks. The Wringham Flats, at Eddington Circus, look tall and hopeful in the manner of the New World constructions of the sixties. Not so long ago, eight people died alone there, within a four-month period. They each lay undiscovered for periods ranging from a few weeks to more than a year. Some of them drank, some of them didn't; most were old, and they didn't go out much or speak to the neighbours. They were away from the world, and everything was away from them. You can see how it happens. Someone loses their family, or loses touch with them. They move into a small flat – maybe via a hostel – and they grow reclusive. You're not seen. London Electricity sends a bill, a reminder, another reminder, a disconnection notice, then a guy comes along and cuts the supply off at the basement. The same with gas; with telephone; with milk, if you have it. Months pass, sometimes years. The flat is self-contained and sealed, the floors are pre-stressed. Nothing comes in, nothing escapes, until someone stumbles in on it. That's mostly how it happens.

'There have always been loners, or people who go off to one side,' Martin said. But he thinks it's got worse for such people, living and dying in these British Isles. He thinks there's a general failure of sympathy, but is even more concerned with the newer mental health legislation ('the obvious failure there'), and even more concerned again with the way housing is sometimes allocated. 'Those high-rise blocks,' he says, 'have made these people's lives more insular. They're all within their own little box, not knowing who's above or below or on either side of them. If you take that sort of building, then start putting *vulnerable* people into these boxes, twenty floors up, then clearly things can get worse.' It's possible to have warden-assisted housing projects, and care worker visits, but that is expensive, and there's not always the money. It's not about fault, or blaming people, it's just one of the things that can happen now. People may go missing within their own community, without ever leaving it. They may be lost, without going anywhere at all. It's just something about the way we live. Outside, people are coming and going all the time, and inside, somewhere indoors, you'll find people just going, or already quietly gone. We go about in the world, leaving traces of ourselves here and there, but there are times when a person's traces will wear away – in the outside places they walked or played in, or even in the rooms they occupied for years – and all you can do then is churn through a bundle of questions, or sapple some stern little likelihoods, and hope it will never be you. Never you, and never yours.

THE SQUARE WAS full of people taking pictures of each other, waiting in line for the cinema. I wanted to see Cathy before it got too dark, before she went to sleep somewhere, or before she got too out of it, in the way that she always did. In the south-easterly corner of Leicester Square, in a temporary cold-weather shelter one floor up, I found her eating a plate of pasta. I sat down beside her, and kept watch. Her eyes were only half-open; her arms were bendy and loose; her head was hovering over the plate, and she coughed. She would smile between mouthfuls, happy enough to be where she was. The room contained a few kids I'd seen elsewhere. Angel, the runaway who loved pop stars, was swinging a padlock over on the other side. She'd fresh scratches on her hands, and a new tattoo across her knuckles: AMAB. She told me later that it stood for 'all men are bastards'.

Cathy looked up, and I gave her a smoke. She'd been missing for two years. Her face had been in the *Big Issue* – in the 'Missing: Can You Help?' column – but she'd gone on doing her own thing, never really hiding from people, just not phoning anyone, or giving her real name. She said she didn't care if anybody knew where she was or not. As we spoke, she smoked one cigarette after another. She was born in Limerick, and moved to Slough when she was two. So she went to school in England – 'absolute shite', she said, shaking her head, fairly disgusted – and suffered through the reputations of her siblings (there are nine of them). She got out of school at sixteen, and headed into London, to King's Cross. She begged and slept out, and didn't know anything about hostels then. 'I didn't sleep much at night,' she said, ' 'cause I thought I was gonna be attacked. I just stayed in little corners, away from everybody, just scared.'

'They didn't know where you were, did they?'

'No, I couldn't go back,' she said, 'too many dodgy memories; the house they were still living in, I didn't wanna live there.' She stayed in a squat in Caledonian Road, and she did

187

some work with the Community Volunteers Service, looking after kids with meningitis, but that all fell through. I asked her what happened.

'It was drugs,' she said. 'I couldn't really get it together.'

'Did you get caught up in drugs at King's Cross?'

'No, when I was fourteen, I used to have panic attacks. They put me on Temazepam. Then there was this thing on the TV about Benzos, saying you could get addicted to them, and they took me off of them, but by then it was too late.'

'Were you swallowing them, or injecting?' I asked.

'Both. I kept on taking them. I just detoxed off of them, but it didn't work. I've just kept buying eggs [Temazepams] and banging them in. I had abscesses on my arms and legs, I went into St Mary's – a mental ward – but I left after a month.'

She went on, and told of what it's like trying to withdraw. Prescription drugs of the Benzodiopate kind are hard to get off. She was back on them – you could see that – and bought as many as ten capsules a day. She'd inject them in doorways, or shop toilets, or places like that. Maybe four or five injections in twelve hours. She's young, and when she's outside, certain characters – offering drugs on tick, or in exchange for favours – will now and then try to get her involved in prostitution, or videos, or 'clipping' (leading a sex client on, taking him round the corner, then letting the pimps beat him up for his money). Cathy tries to keep away from all that now. She's been in debt to these guys in the past. She tells me she wants a simple life, she'd like to be a community worker, and have a family maybe, or something. She wants to do some good, and have some good done to her; she wishes she could stop the drugs, and rejoin the world, but, clearly, it's not just as easy as saying it. She still needs drugs too much.

'I know loads of us,' said Cathy, 'loads of missing persons. You just come away, change your name, change your accent, whatever.' We spoke about that. I said she was only one sort of missing, there were others; some people disappeared and were never found again. There would be people, I said, who thought that was her situation. Children went missing, so did old people, and so did places, and people's stories, and their records, and many things about them. 'Yeah,' she said, 'some of these girls I know, as young as fifteen, they're out of the way, caught up in all sorts, though I know where they are, and they know where to get me.' She scraped back her hair and smiled. 'I didn't just bugger off from a nice little suburban house,' she said, 'or anything. It wasn't like that, it was fucking hard. I was a mess.' She was still coughing and spluttering, and she asked me how she looked.

'You look tired,' I said.

'Dozy, yeah? That's the thing. I feel fine, but I know I look sort of . . . mangled.'

Cathy is going off to Buckinghamshire or somewhere in a day or two; she might stay with a friend she knew years ago. She's been running for years, hiding outside; maybe there's a chance she can gather herself together now. If things don't work out, she says she'll be back here, in London, and that'll be that. 'You can lose yourself, completely, absolutely. You don't have to tell anyone your story, or where you come from; and people just, like, accept that. They think that something's happened and you don't wanna say, and that's it.'

That was the last time I saw Cathy. She may have gone away the next day or the day after, and found a way to make herself better, out there in the country. Or she may have gone somewhere else, or stayed more or less where she was. I couldn't

189

say. All I know is that Cathy was there. I poked my head into the sitting room before I left, and saw her slumped right in front of the shelter's TV, which was showing an old episode of *Rising Damp*. She sat in the big room alone, and I watched her from the door. The beam from the telly screen lit on her face, and her eyes were closed. She was fast asleep. She looked, for all the world, like nothing could harm her now. Nothing could get to her, not even herself.

WESTWORLD

GLOUCESTER WAS VERY QUIET that day, and it rained. Four weeks had passed since the Press first arrived in their black cabs, ready to win. They had moved around easily – professionally – with all the help that comes from gentle banter and loud cheque-books. The journalists had made the most of this one, and the local police were still hopping up and down. But the cabs were gone now, and the local folk were left to contemplate the threat of a normal day. The place felt a little stricken, a little dizzy, as if the shock hadn't quite worn off. And as far as whole places can ever be seen to suffer, then the city of Gloucester I came to that April was hungover and depressed, unsettled, and dispirited. But all in all it suffered quietly: it was like a trampled field once the big top is gone.

The Kings Walk Centre is a mall built round the notion of triangles. As I passed through it that day, I kept looking up at the ceiling, where the triangles were mirrors, and where red and blue neon lights blinked a gruesome hello. The noise volume, for a mall, was way down low. On the ceiling, everyone was marching ahead, upside-down; some had Waitrose bags swinging around them, or double pushchairs out in front; others had toddlers straining at the motherly paw. The sound coming out of the speakers – the musak – seemed more than usually passive-aggressive. And it appeared to have a message: something like Don't Listen to Me, Listen to Yourselves. I listened, though not for long. There was a freezing draught blowing from one end of the Centre to the other. The doors opened at one end, and you could feel it barging in, passing over you, and creeping up the sleeves of your jacket. A yellow card shop beamed over like a smile. The shop was called Someone, Somewhere.

I made off down Eastgate Street, turned right into Wellington Street, and then right again. A hailstorm started up just after I made the turn, and Cromwell Street appeared soaked and blasted. A young woman was pushing a pram against the force of the hail. I stopped beside her, she half smiled, and I bent down to pull a bit of the plastic hood, to cover the baby's face, which was exposed and already a little splashed. 'Is that shorthand?' she said, nodding at the pad under my arm. I shook my head. 'No, just messy writing.' She told me she'd once tried to learn the short stuff. She seemed to know right away why I was there. I asked her what she thought of the discoveries at number 25.

'Oh, don't,' she said, 'I can't bear thinking about those poor girls. It's just terrible. They should knock it down.'

At 25 Cromwell Street a lone policeman stood guard. On the concrete path going from the house to the street, and round the front window, there were bunches of flowers lying about in the puddles. One of the wreaths was made up of

daffodils, in the shape of a cross, with pink ribbon wrapped
around the crossbar. The plastic wrappers on the bouquets
crackled as the wind got up. Number 25 was on three levels
and painted tan. The house next door was all white. On the
other side stood a Seventh-Day Adventist church, presided over
by Pastor I. Lovek. There was a poster behind glass on the side
of the church. 'I am the resurrection and the life,' it read, 'he
that believeth in me though he were dead yet shall he live.' The
words are from John 11: 25, and Pastor Lovek may have
selected them specially, these last few weeks, when the world's
news recordists were pressed hard against his walls. There is a
window on each level at number 25. The frames are painted
green, and each window has a differently patterned net curtain
behind the glass. The front door has a horseshoe above it. An
imitation gas lamp is attached to the wall of the porch; an
electricity wire runs away from it, into the house.

People came by, from time to time, and some would stop to
speak with the policeman. 'No, they've stopped digging for the
weekend,' he says, 'they're having a day off.' A young man and
woman stood behind me for some time, sighing. They shook
their heads. 'Terrible secrets,' the man said eventually. 'Come
on, love, you've seen it now.' The policeman was open and
helpful that day. He seemed to understand people's curiosity,
and he gave them whatever information he could. He was
telling me something about the local area, and about drugs,
when a loud Mancunian voice came rasping from across the
street. 'Oi, mate!' it shouted. I just ignored it for a minute,
until it started shouting, 'Oi, mate, you a reporter?' He was
loud. The cop lifted his eyebrows. I turned round. The guy
was shouting from a first-floor window of the house directly
opposite to the one we were at.

'You a reporter?' he said again. I nodded.

'OK. You want a room? Fifty quid. You'll not get a better view than this.' I laughed then, but was trying to turn down the offer without getting into a big discussion about it. 'No? . . . What? . . . Other folk around here are charging a hundred,' he said, by way of a final pitch. He waited a bit. Then he shrugged and pulled the window down.

When the searches at number 25 were at a peak, early in March 1994, many of the locals and much of the press displayed a sort of mutually exploitative madness. Some of the neighbours made money allowing keen photographers to take snaps over their fence (£50), or from windows looking down at the digging area (£100). The price for bedsit accommodation in the street was high in those first weeks, and most people – taken by surprise by hundreds of cash-happy journalists suddenly relying on them – weren't beyond charging £1 to use the toilet or £3 for a bacon sandwich. People knew it wouldn't last, so they took advantage while they could. It seemed that no one was really thinking about what it all meant.

The rain had gone off a bit, and the windows were starting to glint. I was talking to myself – asking questions, turning things over – as I watched the windows dry at 25 Cromwell Street. I thought about the street name. Gloucester had been a Roundhead city. I looked at the road, stretching down to a park at the end, thinking how standard it was, how like many British streets, with their miserly front gardens and scuffed brick. I tried thinking about what happened here. Nine young women had gone missing. Less than half were reported. Less than half. I had began to wonder about their lives, and to think of others who had lived in this place. It struck me round about there, and then, what had drawn me. I wanted to see this threshold, this gate here. It was one I'd come to again and again, in my head, when writing of the missing girls, and it was one I'd never go through, as they did. I wanted to know something of the girls as they'd been in life. There would be little point in going indoors. I knew that. It wasn't their ending I was after, but something of their beginnings, and perhaps of the middling parts of their lives. I knew, though, that in most cases the beginning and the end weren't at all far apart. There wasn't much middle: they were all quite young. I wanted to know who they were. I wondered what had brought each of them to this front gate, and to other front gates I'd come across myself. I'd walk much too late to find those girls alive; most had died when I was next to nothing, and had lain undiscovered all the years I'd been growing up. I was too late to interrupt their deaths – as you dream sometimes of doing – but perhaps not too late to find something of their lives, something of their time. I was sure, as I stood there, that there must be something to go back to; there had to be more to observe about them, something more than the horrible truths represented by this house and its shiny windows.

I stared at the face of the building as a passerby, with little thought for the rooms and gardens that stretched behind. I wouldn't go there. I thought about this in front of the house, and felt – lost for a second in the brightness – that someone was watching me from inside. Girls had been lost here, that was all that mattered. That was all that remained. Some came here to live; they were happy sometimes, and sometimes miserable, and one day they were murdered. I'm sure none of them expected to die. In many cases, people didn't seem to notice they'd gone. Girls were brought here, and they passed through this gate in some cases hopeful and in others distressed. They were murdered too, and their whereabouts were hidden for twenty years.

I've always thought about people's stories, and their houses, and changing places, and these things have caused me to write this book. But above all, as far as it goes, I've been looking for missing persons, in my own head, for as long as I can remember. And I lost myself in front of those Cromwell Street windows, seeing for the first time (though I should already have known it) that here was the place where such interests might end. They end in loss. This is the real full stop on my search for the missing: the dark, worst, last thing. This is where the unanswerables find their answer; where mystery unravels; where much that was unseen finally makes itself terribly apparent. The missing had always moved – though too much in the corners of my own imagination – in places that might be reducible to the facts of murder and concealment. In a growing mind, though, that can't be all there is; such final facts can't in themselves put an end to the sort of doubts that cause you to seek out explanations of your world. There must be other thoughts, other ways of making sense of things, of unusual events, happening in your very usual world. But murder and concealment sat by, patiently, like hellish twins who had, between them, always known the answer. And now I knew it too. I was here, looking at it.

The path was empty of people, and it was getting a bit late. As I stuffed my things away a woman drew up in a blue car. The car was full of kids. Her hair was blonde, and she got out with a bouquet of flowers in her arms. She came up to the gate. The policeman asked her if she'd like to lay them herself. 'Please,' she said, not loud. He pulled back the barrier and let her walk through. She tiptoed between the other flowers and laid her own bunch under the front window. As she walked back to the car, her head was down, and tears streamed down her face. I had gone over to the other side of the road by this time, and when I turned, I saw her looking at the steering-wheel, her eyes brimming over, while the kids, quite oblivious to everything, went on with their hitting and playing on the back seat.

FIVE WEEKS PREVIOUSLY, on 24 February 1994, police officers went to the semi-detached house at 25 Cromwell Street armed with a search warrant. It was the home of fifty-two-year-old builder Frederick West and his wife Rosemary. They had moved to the house in 1972, and were living there with children Stephen, May, Tara, Louise, Barry, Rosemary, and Lucyanna. Their first daughter, Heather, had been missing since June 1987, when she was aged sixteen. Police had come to the house several times before, and had conducted interviews there two years earlier in relation to Heather's disappearance. Two days after arriving with the warrant, police investigators discovered the remains of a young girl at the back of the garden. They were later identified as those of Heather West. Police continued to excavate at 25 Cromwell Street for the next six weeks, and over the course of that period they discovered eight more sets of remains. All were of young girls who'd been missing for periods going all the way back to 1973.

Searches of the Wests' previous home, at 25 Midland Road, just across the park, resulted in the discovery of the remains of Charmaine West, a little girl who hadn't been seen since 1971. She had been the daughter of Catherine ('Rena') Costello, Frederick West's first wife, who herself had been missing since the late sixties. West had lived with his first wife in the village of Much Marcle, a sparse little place over the border into Hereford and Worcester. Police began digging up a patch called Letterbox Field late in March, and they quickly found the remains of two women. Catherine Costello was one of them, and the second remains were later identified as being those of Anne McFall, a friend of Catherine's from Glasgow, a young woman who has made the trip south with her friend in the mid-sixties, looking for a new life in England.

In the days following the first discoveries at Cromwell Street, calls to the Missing Persons Helpline more than tripled, as mothers and brothers and ex-boyfriends suddenly thought of girls they hadn't seen in years. Missing persons files were dredged for connections; people came forward with last sightings, and memories over twenty years old. A whole group of lives which had long gone unremarked were suddenly opened up. Those girls hadn't gone away and made a better life; they hadn't found love and children; they hadn't cut themselves off, as many thought, or tried to forget. They had been murdered, and their bodies were concealed all the time. Gloucester, and the Britain beyond, seemed suddenly like a kingdom of broken nets, lost connections, social incohesion, and traps. That twelve young women could have gone missing, many so close to their homes, so much in the open, and that they went undiscovered for so long, was one sort of bad news. That many of them were unmissed – unlooked for in any sense – was getting close to the worst sort of news possible. It's the kind of news that never stops being bad, and never stops being news, as there is always the possibility of secrets, of more of the same bad news presently unrevealed, still to come. There are other girls, all over Britain, missing since the late sixties. Their life stories are ill-apparent, their whereabouts are unknown, and news of their deaths can only come as a surprise if it ever comes at all.

Frederick West hanged himself in Winson Green gaol, Birmingham, on New Year's Day 1995. Rosemary West has been charged with ten murders, two counts of rape, and two of assault. She has no connection with the deaths of Rena Costello and Anne McFall. Mrs West maintains her innocence, and says she knew nothing about any of the crimes. She was committed for trial in Dursley Magistrates' Court four weeks after her husband's suicide.

WEST COUNTRY VILLAGES – if we follow Thomas Hardy – have enough tragedy of their own to be going on with, without having to deal with alleged serial killings. At the end of the first day of Rosemary West's committal hearing in Dursley, a big crowd had gathered outside the court. As we filed down the steps, a young woman who'd been sitting in the public gallery drew up beside me. 'Did you see her face?' she said, pushing her tongue between her teeth. I took my place with the mob, or just behind them, next to a tree by the main road. The school-kids were lapping it up; it was carnival time, and no one was for missing it. Two little boys with sticks sniggered and whooped and chased each other round the tree. They both had grey jumpers on, tiny ones, with ST JOSEPH'S R.C. PRIMARY stitched in gold thread. A snapper from one of the cheerier papers had doled out eggs to some of the barrier-huggers. When the van drew out of the yard, with Rosemary West inside, they all went ape. Eggs and sticks bounced off the windows and the mudguards. Expletives rumbled after the van, and a stray BBC reporter – Crombie-coated and bent with the pad – copped a flying egg on the back of the head. Everywhere you looked, it was fury and laughter. Walking along the pavement a few minutes later, I bumped into the Beeb with the egg. 'Yeah, well,' he muttered, 'you can't say the BBC don't get close to the story.'

After seeing the van away that night, I walked up the hill to the Springfields Estate, where Barbara and Bryan lived, and where I had stopped most of the week. Barbara walked with me; she'd been in the court as well, and we were both yawning. It was just about to turn dark, there was a smell of fire, and you could see quite clearly, from the brow of the road, the layers of hill and woodland going all the way down to the Severn. The estate was clean and quiet. 'It's not like Council round here,' said Barbara, 'it was a bit snooty at first, when I was pregnant with Nicola. I mean, a woman needs company at that time, and the neighbours, well, they acted like you were never there.' By the time we got to the door the street-lamps had come on. Someone over the back fence worked in a hospital nearby. She was taking down the details of a woman on one of the wards the other day, she said, and she asked the woman how many children she'd had. 'I had two,' she whispered, 'but one of them was taken.' The patient was the mother of Mary Bastholm, who disappeared in 1984, and whose body is still missing. There is no known connection between Mary and the Wests.

Barbara's house felt quite familiar. The brick fireplace was covered with framed wedding pictures and baby snaps. Everything was soft and fringed; the sofa brown and deep, with a warm newspaper just handy. Knitting-needles and balls of wool were there, and Disney videos stacked behind smoky glass, waiting for the grandkids to come and plug them in. The ceiling, when you tilted back, was covered with Artex fans. All of this worked together, the heat settled, and in seconds I was fast asleep. Later on, I went to get something from my room (still Nicola's room, even though she is married) and I could hear Barbara on her bedroom phone. 'No, Audrey. I tell you, she looks exactly like her picture. Just exactly that.' There was an old Flatly spin-dryer at the foot of my bed, and the walls were covered with Nicola's hairdressing certificates, her City & Guilds. She worked now as a mobile hairdresser and she still kept her perm lotion, her curlers and all her stock under the bed here. Over on the other wall was a board covered with snaps of family nights out, birthdays, and christenings. They were all hugging and kissing and having a good time. Below that was a framed certificate from the Distinguished Service Club of the Royal Mail. It was Bryan's; he'd been a local postman for thirty-five years.

'You read a lot of books?' said Bryan, deep in the sofa. He nodded as I made my excuses. 'Yeah,' he said, 'I'm looking forward to all the books I can read when I'm retired.' He hated the idea of privatization at the Post Office, and didn't want to start asking people for money. He told me more about Dursley, and sketched out his years with Barbara. The whole town surrounded Lister's Engineering Works, but they'd been laying off for years, and it wasn't the place it used to be. 'It never is,' I said cheekily.

'No,' chipped in Barbara, 'it never is. Who's for cha-cha?'

The talk from the courtroom still played in my head as we watched the news. On *Midland Today* there was an item about the arrest of a man in Walsall in connection with the discovery of a skeleton in the garden of his house. The remains were believed to be those of a young girl who lived nearby. She went missing in 1978.

At four thirty the next day Nicola drove me to the station.

Nicola was so happy and pretty, I was sad to leave her. We'd become pals that week, talking about life in the West Country, about writing, and hairdressing. As we drove towards the station I asked Nicola if she ever went out of Dursley to do people's hair. 'Only if they're clients I had before, you know? I mean, you couldn't just go to any house, could you?' I guessed not. As the car drew into the station yard, she told me that nothing much ever happened in Dursley.

On the train back to London, head against the window, I began turning over all that I'd learned since those first visits to Cromwell Street, which I'd made almost exactly one year before. Meetings in Gloucester and Glasgow jumbled in my head; documents and pictures and conversations fluttered about, and I began the process of piecing some of the lives together. I closed my eyes, and made my way back to the start.

CATHERINE COSTELLO WAS born in Coatbridge, outside Glasgow, on 14 April 1944. Her family lived then at 218 Calder Street. Her father, Edward Costello, worked in a local scrap-iron yard, and her mother, Mary, stayed home to look after Catherine and her sisters. Edward's father had been a coalminer in Coatbridge all his life. Edward's first wife died young, and he married Mary when he was thirty-four. She had been married before too, to a brickmaker called William Denmark, who came from the Baillieston area of Glasgow. Mary's family had lived not far from there, at 537 Old Shettleston Road, and she was working in an engineering factory when she married Denmark at the age of seventeen. But that first marriage didn't work out, and they were divorced after a few years. She'd gone back to live at her family's home in the thirties, and it was then that she met Edward Costello, whom she wed just after Christmas 1936, with her young sister Isabella Gibson standing as her witness.

Catherine was always known as Rena. She was quite restless from an early age; it was as if she couldn't wait to get out and get on with things. She left school at fifteen and worked here and there, on buses and in shops. Rena wasn't loud or brash, but she was unsettled, and sometimes impulsive. She would gather a reputation as a bit of a goer – she was one for a drink, and a good time – though all she seemed to want in the end was to have kids and a tolerable life. In the spring of 1962, she was working as a conductress on one of the bus routes around Bishopbriggs. She went out with one of the drivers, an Asian man, and she fell pregnant. There was no future with the guy, and she didn't want to be amongst her own people, so she turned her attention once again to ideas of getting out, getting away, and getting on with her own life. One of her sisters had a connection in England – in Hereford or Gloucester or something – and Rena decided to go there and give it a try. There was no guarantee, but she'd see how it all worked out.

She got a job that summer working as a waitress in a Herefordshire put – the New Inn, in Ledbury. This part of the country, like many at the time, was undergoing a fair bit of change. A lot of the old agricultural work was being supplemented by new instruments factories. Manufacturing jobs were all the rage, and a few modern housing developments were beginning to spring up here and there, out on the edges of the traditional villages with their central clocktowers. Rena was a sweet-looking girl. It was too early in the decade for the dark, smooth beehive and thick eyeliner that many would later remember as her trademarks. She still had a fifties look in

Ledbury: the hair was bleached blonde, was styled wavy, and the dresses were frilly but neat. She met a man that summer. He had dark curly hair, nice teeth, and wore a collar and tie. He was quite handsome; he looked a bit wild, like a gypsy. He was a worker, though, a hard worker, this man Fred West.

Rena told Fred that she was pregnant, and he didn't seem to mind. She told friends back in Glasgow that he was all for the idea at first. They got married. But maybe he changed his mind about the pregnancy over Christmas, for Rena moved back to Coatbridge in the new year, and went to live at 46 Hospital Street. She went from there to the Alexander Hospital on the afternoon of 22 March 1963, and she gave birth to a daughter that evening. She called her Mary. Rena was still living in Coatbridge in September, but she'd applied for a Glasgow corporation house, and she was to be offered one early in 1964. In the meantime, there was the baby's christening, which took place at St Mary's Roman Catholic Church in Coatbridge on 6 September. Fred had come to Scotland around that time. Either Rena or Fred, or both together, didn't like the original choice of name for the baby. So it was changed from Mary West to Charmaine Carol Mary West.

When the new home came up, the three of them moved into it together. The flat was on the ground floor of a tenement at 25 Savoy Street, in the Bridgeton area of Glasgow. The tenements of Bridgeton – like those of Calton, and Dalmarnock, the near neighbourhoods – were mostly torn down in the late sixties and in the seventies. Savoy Street was in a state of dilapidation in 1964, and Fred and Rena were among the last people to live there before it was torn down. The house they lived in was a two apartment, known there and then as a 'room and kitchen'. The murky back-courts were used for washing and drying, and it was here you'd find the middens – the bins – which sometimes doubled as an ashpit.

Many of the families who'd lived here were moved out to the new housing estates – Castlemilk, Easterhouse, Milton – in the fifties; some others had moved into the newer cottage-style houses going up here and there in the area. But the really final demolition went ahead in the seventies, when you'd see street corners marked only by a single ripped tenement, waiting for the final work to be done. There would, for a time, be giant gap-sites and piles of rubble where there used to be life, albeit tenement life. A whole way of living was eventually wiped away – and most were more glad than sentimental about it – in the years between 1964 and 1979. This is one of the areas in Glasgow sometimes referred to as a Goner. Old pictures, and local histories, show a Bridgeton altogether different. They show the area my grandfathers lived next to, and knew very well. They show houses my parents visited, and shops they used. They show the carriage-hirer which features in the Sinn Fein outrage of 1921. And they show cinemas – Green's, the Strathclyde in Summerfield Road, the Olympia, the Premier in Kilpatrick Street, known locally as 'the Geggie' – places that no longer exist, not even as names, though the old street names remain much the same, whilst all around is different.

This was the world the West family found themselves moving into early in 1964. Savoy Street was connected to Bridgeton Main Street by the Savoy Arcade, a pend which ran under and between two tenements at the middle. There was a small factory, a sweet-making concern, that stood across from the old pend, next to the tenement at number 25. It was let by Alfred and Charles Ellsworth. They made a really popular west coast of Scotland sweetie, the 'MB' bar. There was a would-be gangster at number 16 – Billy Beck – who was known around the local area as the Bandit. He was a wiseguy, a blow-hard, a petty crook, and he was one of those characters who people would say was 'into everything'. He was the kind of guy who'd hand out pound notes to the kids playing in the street, then swagger back to his house wondering how he was going to make it through the rest of the week.

Savoy was an intimate street, as most of those old ones were, but it was a place where you could get on with your life in peace if you wanted to. You could gauge how much you cared to be involved in neighbourhood affairs, in the life of the area, and take your chances if you involved yourself too much. But Rena and Fred didn't mix a great deal. He didn't mix at all, in fact. They were both pretty quiet, private even. Fred got a job as an ice-cream salesman. The van he drove was called Mr Whippy, and was rented from Walls' Ice-Cream, who had a main yard in Paisley. He worked all hours of the day, and well into the night, taking his van around the local areas.

Archie and Mary Jackson lived across the landing. They had three young girls, and had moved to Savoy Street not long before the Wests, buying their flat for under £400. Archie was a welder, working with A & S Constructors in Shawfield. He worked for seventeen years with the same firm, doing seven days a week and a lot of overtime. He was friends with Robert Murdoch, who lived round the corner at 70 Reid Street, just down from Mary's parents. Robert's uncle Bobby was the same Bobby Murdoch who used to play for Celtic. The Brannigan family lived on the first floor at number 25, in the flat above the Wests. Alex Brannigan at that time drove a grocery van around the city, and it was his brother who bought the Jacksons' flat once they decided to move out. It was a good close, very friendly, and nobody would interfere too much with anybody else.

Archie Jackson maintains – though others from the time think differently – that Fred West wasn't around Savoy Street much, if at all. He remembers Rena very well, and has a memory of an old woman, an old dear with an Irish accent who Rena called 'auntie'. She was in and out of Rena's flat all the time, but not Fred. Fred may well only have come and gone from the flat. But he was certainly there sometimes. Rena gave birth to their daughter Anna Marie on 6 July, and it was Fred who signed the birth certificate, giving the family address as 25 Savoy Street. Some pictures turned up too, of little Anna Marie, only a few weeks old, being held by her mother in front of an ice-cream van. The van is parked in Savoy Street.

Archie remembers Charmaine and Anna Marie playing outside the window. One was very dark: the older one. Rena seemed really nice. She was clean, she wasn't a pest. 'It wasn't,' said Archie, 'as if her knuckles were bleeding wi' chappin' at yer door.' She only ever came into the Jacksons' flat once. It was Hogmanay, and she came over and had a drink with them. Archie remembers her as being very young. He went over to her house for something that night, but he can't remember what it was. He thinks he might have been going over to check on the kids, or get a bottle, or something. But that was the only time. Rena seemed quite contented then; she didn't have sore faces or anything like that. The Jacksons decided to emigrate to Canada, and, before long, they said goodbye to the young girl next door and her two wee kids dressed exactly the same. When they came back to Glasgow, seven years later, Savoy Street was gone.

ANNE MCFALL WAS five years younger than Rena. She was born at the maternity hospital at Rottenrow on 8 April 1949. She was brought from the hospital to her mother's house in Parkhead. The address was 30 Malcolm Street. Her father was Thomas McFall, a motor mechanic, and her mother was Jeannie Hunter, who worked during the day cleaning people's houses. Jeannie didn't like her husband, and Anne grew up to dislike him as well. She was all for her mother. It seems that Anne – and perhaps her mother, too – never really knew the true story of Thomas McFall. He left them with nothing, though he would appear on the scene from time to time, trying to rearrange their lives, and causing trouble. It is easier for us to consider the facts than it must have been for them. Primary among them was the fact that Jeannie and Thomas were never married, though Anne's friends assumed that they were. He was actually married to somebody else, a woman called Christina Drummond, and he had been since October 1930. His first home with his real wife was a tenement flat at number 6 Savoy Street, Bridgeton. They were still married when Thomas died in 1968.

Jeannie never had it easy. She had, in fact, what you might readily consider to have been a terrible life. She was lied to for years, and it was the sort of lying that would cause her to lie to herself as well, just to make things seem better. She lived one of those Glaswegian lives that involved the sort of poverty many of us would only hear about, and think mythical. It was a life lived on the rebound; one where she was forced – and forced by herself – to dwell at the centre of a brutal man's rage and disappointment. She would be beat-up, and she'd breed a son who'd come to turn on her as well. She had little for herself, and she retreated into drink fairly young. But Anne was everything she lived for. Her daughter was beautiful, and she thought there was nobody like her mother.

Anne's brother was known in the area as Scarface McFall.

He was never out of the gaol. He was away so much, in fact, that all Anne's friends thought he was dead. He'd been murdered in a gang fight, they thought, and some would even tell you the street he'd been killed in. Malcolm Street was tucked in just underneath Parkhead Stadium, the home of Celtic Football Club. Anne went to school at St Michael's, and she was friendly with a girl who lived at 48 Malcolm Street, a girl called Isa. Anne was a Catholic and Isa a Protestant, but it made no difference to them, they were firm friends. They were both desperate to get out of school, to go off and earn some money, and they each left at the first opportunity: first Isa, then Anne. They worked beside each other at a place called Livingston Industrial Clothing, at the bottom of Dalmarnock Road, next to the train depot. They sat together on the production line, machine-sewing the necks onto polo-necks. The two girls would often spend their bus fare on fags, and walk to work full of talk about boys and the good life to come.

In 1965 Isa and Anne started going to the Victoria Café in Scotland Street. Isa had met a guy who she liked; he was one of those who marched in the Orange Walk, and he lived just across from the café in Cowie Street. The girls met Rena Costello in the café. Rena was a good laugh. She had two kids; the youngest, whom they were calling Anna Marie, was still in her pram. The girls and Rena clicked right away. They would meet in there often after that, sharing cigarettes and money, and talking of the troubles they had. But they laughed more than anything else. Rena's husband was always out with his ice-cream van, so she really came and went as she pleased.

Fred and Rena had moved out of the flat in Savoy Street early in 1965, and had taken a flat at the very end of McLellan Street in Kinning Park. It was on the first floor left, at number

241. The street was long, but it only had houses on one side – the other side was taken up almost completely by the McLellan Steel Works. After knowing Isa for a few months, Rena asked her to come to live in McLellan Street, and help her and Fred look after the children. Fred tended to call her a nanny, just as he'd later say that of Anne, when she took on the job, replacing Isa. But it was really just an excuse for the unmarried girls to get away from Malcolm Street. There wasn't much in the way of official duties.

Fred started to hit Rena around this time. He'd go out in his van in the afternoon and he wouldn't come back until three or four in the morning. He'd sometimes come back in a state of agitation, and he'd pull Rena out of bed, beat her, and shout the place down. Fred went back to Gloucester for short periods during the year; he seems to have taken the kids away for a spell in March. He asked the local authority in Much Marcle to take them into care. Then, for whatever reason, he brought them back to Glasgow. Isa said he was a 'Jekyll and Hyde'. He could just turn.

There was a young man who lived at 94 McLellan Street with his wife. His name was John McLachlan. His best pal at the time was Norrie Mason, who lived in the flat below Fred and Rena West at the end of the street. The pals would often go to the betting shop, Telky's, which sat right next door to Norrie's close. Sometimes they'd get a carry-out, a few cans of lager, and a half bottle, and take it up to Norrie's flat to drink. They came in one afternoon and saw Norrie's wife Sarah sitting on the sofa next to a pretty young woman with a beehive hair-do. The girl was nice looking, with a bright smile. It was Rena. The men opened the cans, split the seal on the whisky, and they all had a drink together. John remembers seeing a face at the window, a dark face, a head of curly hair, and he opened the door to see who it was. It was Fred. He came charging in and grabbed Rena, and pulled her up the stairs. He was belting her on the way up.

Rena started going down to the bookie's when she knew John was in there. Some of the girls would try to discourage her – it would drive Fred mad; and, anyway, John was probably just using her. They sometimes went to the park together and, one time, Fred followed them in, and lunged at Rena, battering her from behind. John McLachlan says he set about Fred, beating him up, and that Fred scratched his stomach with a knife. Others stand testament to the fighting – they were always fighting over Rena – but no one knew anything about knives. Rena told Isa she didn't care if Fred was angry about her friendship with McLachlan or not; Rena was sure that Fred, out with his ice-cream van, was up to the same sort of thing. She said that's why she did it: she was cheesed off with Fred's messing about. Isa had began an affair with McLachlan's friend John Trotter, and the four of them – John, Rena, Isa, and John – would go down to the Victoria Café, or to pubs along Paisley Road West.

They were having a good time. It was the right time to be having a good time in Glasgow. The city was opening up to modern things, to new designs, and was partaking of the general swing. Donovan topped the bill at the Glasgow Odeon in May; Herman's Hermits were playing the Barrowland in July; the Stones followed soon after. The Scottish papers were full of Harold Wilson's meeting with Pope Paul at the Vatican; with news of the expansion of John Brown's shipyard on the Clyde (responding to a warning that they should 'modernize or die'; Angie Dickinson made a guest appearance on *Dr Kildare*; and local reports spoke of former British middleweight champion

John 'Cowboy' McCormack making his comeback by beating Bernard Quillier of France in six rounds at Govan Town Hall.

Anne McFall had a boyfriend for a while. He drove a fork-lift truck. She wasn't very interested in him, though, and she wriggled out of it. He then had a terrible accident at his work: he got electrocuted and later died. Anne couldn't bear to think about it. She still spent a lot of time trying to look after her mother. Jeannie wouldn't eat. There was never anything around the house – maybe a half-tin of beans or something like that – and she wasn't eating at all well. Anne worried about her all the time. But there was something else on her mind as 1965 progressed. It was Fred: she thought she was falling in love with him. She'd tell Isa she really liked him, no she loved him, and she knew that Rena didn't. She admitted that she'd do anything he told her to do.

Neighbours in McLellan Street remember Fred West always being out late at night. He was always out with the van. McLellan Street is another of those streets that was swept away in the seventies. Most of it was dismantled to make way for the new M8. But in the street as it was in 1965 there existed, at the far end, an area given over to residential plots. Most people grew vegetables there, or had benches and swings. They were little garden plots. Fred would sometimes go up there after his work. He wasn't a grower, say the neighbours, but he'd often go there. They just thought he was a loner. Sometimes he'd be sociable; he'd invite McLachlan and Trotter and Norrie and some other men over to play cards. But often, halfway through the evening, his mood would turn quite black, and he'd leave them. They'd often find out, the next day, that he'd beaten Rena up after they had gone. There was something not right in McLellan Street.

*

THIRTY YEARS ON, I wanted to speak to John McLachlan. I knew he'd been friendly with Rena, and that he'd gone out in the ice-cream van with Fred, and I needed some detail from him. A Glasgow journalist I spoke to couldn't get to his files, then he was busy writing about national identity cards, then he was off to see Scottish Opera. But he gave me a clue before the phone went down. I thought McLachlan was in the Milton area of Glasgow now, but what street? He considered it a moment, then said that he thought it was a place called Vallay Street.

Trying to find people to talk to about missing persons is a little like looking for missing persons themselves. I have a real handicap: I'm OK face to face, but I can't stand speaking to people I don't know on the telephone. I'll do anything to avoid it. If there's no name and address in the telephone book – McLachlan was ex-directory – I'll go for the voters' rolls, so long as I have a street name. I raided for stuff about streets old and new, and found other names, unexpected ones, that made me think, once again, that there are more ways to be missing than the obvious ways. Telling my story of missing persons forever brings me back to the problems and procedures of reportage.

John McLachlan wasn't expecting me. I didn't have his number the first time, and I just hoped he'd be in, and be the right one, and be willing to speak about a woman he knew three decades before. Milton is in the north-west of Glasgow, just beyond Possilpark and Springburn. Rainbow-painted tower-blocks stand like giant exclamation marks over rows of older houses. It is a poor place, and a rough one. Of the ten thousand or so people who live on the estate, nearly four thousand are described in the last census as being 'economically inactive'. That refers to the young and the old, and also to the fact that there's no work. There's a lot of sickness there, too, of one sort and another: over two thousand of those on the estate suffer from long-term illness. It's also full of white Glaswegians. There are only eight black folk there, one Indian, and five Asians. You can buy tranquillizers easily; many youngsters use them in place of heroin.

John's daughter opened the door, and brought me into the living-room. Right away, it was obvious that Mr McLachlan, deep in his chair, was one of the long-term ill. He was surrounded by bottles of pills, and I noticed right away the scars across his bare stomach. I told him who I was; he told me to sit down. 'You might've fuckin' warned me, for fuck's sake,' he said, right away. It surprised even me, the notion that this was somehow easier than talking on the telephone, but it was, and it somehow made sense to come. He began the story of his first meeting with Rena, his fighting with Fred, his memories of little Charmaine and Anna Marie, and descriptions of good times long past, times spent in cafés and pubs with Rena and their friends. He had tattoos all the way up his arms. Some were home-made, some were done professionally. There was a fading one on his left forearm, just above his wrist a little word. It said *Rena*.

John felt that Rena had been looking for someone to cling to in McLellan Street. She had her friends – Isa was always there to babysit and Anne McFall was around the house more and more. But Rena liked male company, and sometimes John would drive her up to his mother's in his green Ford Zephyr, or out to the countryside. It was quite a sexual thing, but he says it took him a while to get into that. 'I was still married, and I didn't know what to do. I thought it was quite dodgy.' John's wife at the time was called Rosie, and his dalliance with

Rena contributed to their final break-up. Rosie was at the window one afternoon as John and Rena strode past, arm-in-arm. At that time Rena had begun to tell John about Fred, about how he'd become obsessed with sex and stuff. She said that to Isa as well and Isa thought he was a 'weirdo'. I asked John about the ice-cream van. 'Aye,' he said, 'he knew a lot of the women. He'd talk to them, and fanny about. He would be away till all hours. Most of the drivers brought their van back at eleven or twelve, but he was out in his till three or four in the morning.'

He lit another cigarette. 'The police came up here last year, and I said to them, "You know what you should do? You should go back to the police station, check up on all the missing lassies about Anne McFall's age, and check if any of them went missing when he was doing his business up here." So they came back up and said, "Do you know these four lassies?" I wasn't sure. One name rung a bell. But it's hard to be sure.' We spoke about the plots at the end of McLellan Street, about just what part of the motorway now went over it, then we left it. John said when he saw the stuff in the papers, the pictures of Fred West and the dead girls of Cromwell Street, he knew right away. Many who knew Rena, and some who'd known Anne, thought the same thing. As soon as the stuff came on the telly, they thought the worst.

On the shelf over John's telly there were boxing trophies awarded to his sons. And there was a giant framed picture of his young daughter. As we talked about the lives of the girls he knew in 1965 and '66 – filling in gaps, finessing names and dates, and homing in on squabbles and journeys and other events – he called my attention to several more recent losses. He pointed to two framed pictures on top of the fireplace. One was of his sixteen-year-old nephew who'd drowned at Loch Lomond. He'd swum in to retrieve a ball and got caught in the current. The other picture was of another nephew who'd hanged himself just four weeks before. He'd gone over to a tree in Milton Park and just hanged himself, in the middle of the afternoon. 'It's hard,' John said, 'it's hard to think about things that happened all those years ago. Rena just wanted to live in peace, with her kids. That was all she ever wanted.'

IN THE AUTUMN of 1965, it became obvious that Fred wanted to get away from Glasgow. He wanted to be back among his own people, and he wanted better things for Anna Marie. People had begun to notice how he didn't care much for Charmaine. Isa had seen how strict he was with the kids, but he'd always relent with Anna Marie, his own daughter. It was Charmaine, along with Rena, who bore the brunt of his temper. One of Rena's friends remembers Charmaine being lifted into the ice-cream van, just a toddler, and her reaching for an ice. Fred slapped her face. The children slept in bunk beds, but not one on top of the other, like you'd expect. Each had a set of bunks of their own, but each child was kept on the bottom bed. Fred had covered the spaces between the top and bottom bunks with something like mesh, made from the ribs from a cot. He'd rigged it all up specially, to keep them in. He demanded that they be kept there: fed, and changed, and forced to play there, as well as sleep. Anne and Isa called it 'the gaol', and they'd lift the children out as soon as the van had turned the corner.

Anne's brother was back living with his mother, and he was making a show of his violent self. He would steal Anne's money from her, taunt her, and worry their mother. Rena and Isa hadn't seen Anne for a while. Fred had gone back down to Gloucester by himself. He went down to get a job and to set up a new home. He told them all that there would soon be a house ready. He said he had found one where they could all live together, but they'd later find out that he'd just made the story up. Anne heard they were planning to go down; she came back onto the scene at McLellan Street not long before they left. Isa wanted to give it a go in England, and Anne did too. It's fair to say that Anne might have had additional motive, but they both agreed that they might get better jobs down south, make a bit of money, and have a laugh at the same time. They wanted to better themselves. It seems that Rena didn't want to go – she'd been down that way before, and come back – but it looked like there wasn't a great deal of choice. Fred had already contacted the Corporation and was ready to give up the house keys. And Rena's short fling with John McLachlan had sort of fizzled out. The feeling wasn't really there on his part, some felt it never had been, though it was clear they would remain friends, and maybe they'd get together now and then.

Fred came to get Rena, Isa, and the two kids in the early hours of the morning. It was agreed that Anne would come down four or five days later, under her own steam. It turned out they were not going to live in a big house at all, but a caravan, and Fred said they could only put Anne up until she got a job and then a place of her own. Anne was still very keen to come, and she went to Malcolm Street to draw herself together. The van Fred drove the others down in was disgusting. His new job was in an abattoir, and the van was full of hides and stinking bones. The girls all sat in the back, surrounded by all this, and chatted non-stop on the way down. They arrived in the village of Much Marcle that afternoon. It was a large caravan park they came to, with hundreds of trailers, but theirs wasn't that big. They got everything set up for themselves in no time. Anne let them know when she was arriving, and they drove over in the horrible van to pick her up at the station.

Rena and Fred had a room of their own, right at the end of the caravan. Charmaine and Anna Marie slept in a small room in the middle, in little beds that you pulled out of the wall. Across from that there was a kitchen, with taps and a basin. There was a table built in just to the side of that, with couches going round it in the shape of a U. Isa slept on the couch on one side, and Anne slept on the other. The two nannies made money by babysitting for as many parents on the site who needed them. They never got far enough off the caravan site to find real work, and they weren't close enough to any big town to see anything, so they just babysat. Though it was money they were after, people would seldom give it to them. They'd pay them in cigarettes, and let them eat what they wanted from the fridge. That was it.

Rena was a sort of prisoner in the caravan. Fred would go to work, which was quite close, and he'd come back every break he had. She'd always to be there. And the girls, though they were allowed to take the children around the park, weren't allowed to take them outside. They'd all to stay nearby. It was like 'the gaol' all over again, and not just for the children. Fred's violence towards Rena had worsened. It was becoming more and more regular, and the beatings were harsher. Sometimes the nannies couldn't stand it, and they'd take the two kids over to a neighbouring caravan till the beating stopped. All the near neighbours knew it was going on; you couldn't fail to notice, you could hear it. This went on for a few months.

There was a lane at the end of the caravan site, with a phone next to it, and one day Isa went down there and phoned the Victoria Café. She left a message for John McLachlan, telling him to phone her at that number at a certain time. He got the message, and rang back. Isa asked him to come and get her and Rena and the weans on the first available weekend he had. They wanted back to Glasgow. They told him a day and a time when they knew Fred would be at work. It was all sorted. But Anne couldn't hold back; she told Fred everything. She grassed up the whole plan, to go back, and to take the kids without him knowing. He came in early from work on the afternoon it was due to happen. The two Johns – McLachlan and Trotter – had come in a hired Mini coupé. They started fighting with Fred, arguing and pushing, as he wouldn't let go of the kids. Fred got the local policeman involved – a bobby on a bike – and the Johns stood back. Rena appealed to Fred to let her take the children. He was spitting fury, and wouldn't let her near them. Anne McFall stood beside the window of the caravan with Anna Marie in her arms. She was slowly shaking her head. Her hair was long and dark, parted in the middle, and her teeth protruded, in the way that they always had since she was a baby herself. Isa pleaded with Anne to come away. Rena, and the Johns too, all of them tried to get her to come with them. They'd make room in the car for all of them. Just leave him, Anne. But no, she hung on, cradling Anna Marie in her arms for all she was worth.

That was the last time Isa saw her childhood friend. For a year or so afterwards, back in Glasgow, when Isa went up to see her own people in Malcolm Street, she'd often bump into Jeannie, Anne's mum, and Jeannie would call Isa in to see the letters and pictures that had come from young Anne in England. The letters were always written nicely, telling of the fantastic job she had, the beautiful big house, and the terrific guy she'd met, a man who loved her, and who was looking after her. She'd enclose photographs of the house. Isa knew it was only a few yards, but a million miles, from the caravan Anne shared with Fred West.

Rena had cried all the way back to Glasgow the day they ran away. She couldn't stand the idea of being without the kids. She told Isa it wasn't so much Anna Marie, she knew she'd be all right with Fred. It was Charmaine. She wasn't sure she'd done the right thing; she hadn't expected a fight. They arrived in Glasgow late that night. McLachlan hadn't separated from his wife yet, and Trotter was still with his mother, so Isa and Rena spent the night in the car. The next day, the girls managed to get a room-and-kitchen flat in Arden Street, Maryhill. They lived there together for a few months. Rena was pining for the children all the time, and she might have pined even harder if she'd known that Fred was trying once again to get the kids taken into care. They were finally taken away, albeit temporarily, in December.

By that time Rena had moved into a bigger house on the other side of Arden Street. Isa was serious about John Trotter by then, and she decided to move back to her parents' house after they got engaged; she had a job in Peacock's Bakery in Duke Street. Around the same time Rena started working as a conductress for Glasgow Corporation buses. Some say she then got in with a pretty rough crowd. There was gossip on the buses about the sort of houses she was spending her time in. It's difficult to know any more than that. It is never easy to write from gossip – none of it squares up to any particular date; little of it squares with other versions. The reliables say that Rena was floating a bit in Arden Street; she was troubled, and was missing the girls. Isa was due to marry John Trotter, and the date was set for 23 July 1966. A few weeks before the date, Rena asked Isa if she'd come back to Much Marcle to help her get Charmaine and Anna Marie. Trotter wouldn't allow it, and Isa told Rena she'd have to go down there herself. Rena thought she'd no choice, and she promised to be back in time for the wedding. Someone who saw her on the buses just before she left Glasgow says it was unclear whether she was giving up the Arden Street house or what. She just went south.

Isa never heard anything more. The wedding went ahead without Rena. Everybody knew she'd probably gone back with Fred, to try and make a go of it with the girls. Her friends felt for her; they knew she would never have an easy life with him, and neither would Charmaine. But they were with him now, and there was no point interfering. In time, lost in the trials of their own lives, they forgot all about them. Rena had never really got on that well with her own family. Most of them didn't want to know her, and they never enquired after her. Anne McFall had never given her family her real address. She was in a grand thatched cottage, as far as they knew. But the letters stopped coming in 1967. Jeannie, her mother, died on 10 February 1969, of malnutrition. People said she couldn't really live without Anne to look after her. She was fifty-nine.

Rena Costello and Anne McFall were never reported missing. Those who knew them hadn't seen their faces for three decades, and when they did see them – smiling from newspapers and television screens during Easter 1994 – they noticed that they hadn't changed in the slightest. They appeared just as they'd known them. They were two faces from the past, two girls from another time, who other people, most people now referring to their names, never thought of as having proper stories of their own. They were just two girls who got killed. But the girls did have stories; they each had one. It's just that their stories came to some sort of brutal, unknown, premature end, and their bodies were hidden under earth for a very long time. The bodies were buried so that nobody would notice – in the hope that no one would – and nobody did. It would appear to the world as if that was the point of them, that was their purpose: as featureless, unwitting ciphers in the early career of a serial killer. But Rena and Anne had, by turns, the biggest and smallest of lives, just like everybody else. They weren't born victims, they were turned into them. They were buried in Letterbox Field, Much Marcle, some time before the end of 1970. Anne was eight months pregnant when she died.

When I finally tracked down Isa, she still bore the home-made tattoos she and her friends had given each other in the mid-sixties, before making their bid for a new life in Gloucester-shire. She showed me them in the house where she'd lived now for fourteen years. It was hard to believe it. Her house was in the place where my immediate family had made their own bid for the better life. She was there in Irvine, on the Bourtreehill Estate, little more than a couple of hundred yards from where young Sandy Davidson had gone missing during that unforget-table spring of 1976.

THE WELLINGTON ARMS is the nearest pub to Cromwell Street; it stands just round the corner. It was loud with talk, and with buzz from the fruit machine, four or five Saturdays after the digging began. I got a bottle of beer and sat at a table near the door. Manchester United were playing Blackburn Rovers on the telly. Someone turned the sound up: all you could hear now was the roar of the crowd and the chiming in of the commentator. 'Kenny Dalglish,' the voice said, 'and Alex Ferguson – the two men from Glasgow – can't hide their dislike of each other here today.' There was a black guy at a table just over the way, a table stacked with cigarettes and bitter, who was having trouble hiding his dislike for most of those around him. But I had cause to think he felt especially badly disposed towards me. His mad stare made me think so. He waved me over.

'You got enough?' he said, pointing to a bag at my side full of notepads and tapes. I didn't know I was that obvious, but I just shrugged. He was sitting with a much smaller guy. I went over to them. The second one was drunk and compliant. He was superior too, full of dickhead winks and warnings, like he was the only one who could possibly save you. Before I was in the seat I'd already been told, by Mr Big, that they had the real story. 'I'm your main man,' he said, 'I've got the big story and a video to go with it.' I tried to get him to explain. 'No, I knew Fred West. I'm talking money, real money. How much will your paper pay for my story?' I just laughed at first, but he pressed me, tapping me on the shoulder every time I turned to look at the TV: 'How much?' I told him my paper didn't have any money; I said that if it did, I'd ask them to pay. He looked wary. 'I'm king of this pub,' he said, 'I could have you thrown out.' He tapped me again on the shoulder: 'But for now you're all right.'

His seconder started telling me about a guy he worked with, a guy in his factory, who got offered £50,000 by the *News of the World* for his story on Fred West. 'What did he do?' I asked.

'He wanted them to up it to six hundred thousand,' he said.

'They negotiated. I don't know what he knew, but he didn't know half of what Leroy knows. Leroy's got the video.'

'What video?'

'Oh, I can't say. He's got it though. You should talk to your paper and get them to pay him for it. I told him, I did, I said, "Bide your time, Leroy – you'll get your money." '

I don't know if Leroy ever did get his money. He blabbed some of the story to me later on, after I bought him a pint, and it was only sensible in parts. He was just blethering – as many were – and most of what he said was irrelevant or untrue. Police had removed cassettes from the house in Cromwell Street near the beginning of the investigation, but it was still not proven that they had any bearing on the circumstances of the case. The situation in the Wellington, though, turned out to be a fairly common one. Everyone had a story; everybody knew something; any minute now the lid would be blown off, and so on. The newspapers encouraged it by printing special phone numbers that 'witnesses' could call and be rung back on. Several people I spoke to had rung the number thinking it was the police. That was how the ads were framed: 'Did you know Fred West? You might have important information relating to our enquiries . . .' The police were constantly troubled by this, by reporters getting to witnesses before they did. Several 'stars' of the case – including Anna Marie West – were contracted to a single newspaper, though this was not in itself seen to interfere with police procedures.

You'd meet people everywhere who had stories to tell, who had theories too, but they were almost always stories to do with the alleged murderers – almost always based around the tabloid fixation on mutilation and sex: they were never stories about the victims' lives. From the village of Much Marcle in the forties (where Fred West grew up) and the Devon of the fifties (where Rosemary Letts grew up) there was a trail of stories and informers, of key-holders and soothsayers, all of them ready with an urgent profile, a telling detail from the pram, a life-changing incident from an ancient building site. The trail led all the way to places like the Wellington Arms. Here the people read the papers, and tried to sell them stories. They got involved by saying they were involved. They spoke of tapes, they analysed the alleged killers' habits, they knew – though they might not have known that they knew it – how the interest being shown in the tragedy was essentially porno-graphic. Everyone was still preoccupied with the nature of the alleged killers; the nature of the killed was never of interest, it was never in much doubt. They were the *victims*. They used to be missing people, and now they were dead.

I came from the Wellington and crossed the park. Just up from a B&Q superstore, jutting off Trier Way, there sits a row of tall, semi-detached houses in a place called Midland Road. I walked up and down the street for a bit, just to see what it was like. They were nice houses. One of them housed the Association of Ukrainians in Britain (Gloucester Branch). I could see, when I got to it, that number 25 was empty. Number 25: the same house number the West family had when they lived in Cromwell Street. This building, in Midland Road, had been the family's first house – they lived here for a short time in the early seventies: Fred, Rena's two children, and Fred's new woman. Some of it was boarded up, and the handle had been removed from the front door. There were three bell-but-tons up the side and a canopy over the door, painted black. The building has two storeys with an attic third. There are six steps up to it. I walked round the back of the house. The grass had got out of control, and there was rubble – loose bricks and chopped wood – strewn around the place. The grass was very long. I looked up at the building. Just then a man came round from the side, a policeman. He'd a white shirt and black tie on but no helmet. He asked me if I could stay round the front; he was keeping guard on the house from a car across the way. I followed him round and asked him when they were due to start digging here. 'Not long,' he said, 'maybe a couple of weeks.'

A LOT OF the shops on Bishop's Cleeve Green would do home deliveries. Smith's the newsagent would bring newspapers, tobacco, and sweets if you ordered them, and Badham's Pharmacy, in Church Road, would open up when required to. Bishop's Cleeve, at the close of the sixties, was that sort of place. In some respects it still is. The village sits at the foot of Cleave Hill, the highest peak in the Cotswolds, and it lies three miles north of Cheltenham on the road to Evesham. From the top of the hill you can see the Vale of Evesham and the Severn, and right in the distance you'll see the Malvern Hills. You can also see the caravan parks for miles around, of which there are many.

Fred West was driving a lorry in 1969, and he'd known Bishop's Cleeve since he was a boy. He met a fifteen-year-old girl in the village called Rosemary Letts early in that year. She lived there with her mother Daley, her father William, an electrician, and the six other Letts children. Rose was born in Barnstaple, in Devon, and the family moved to Bishop's Cleeve in 1964. She started to visit Fred in his caravan, soon after that first meeting. His trailer was, by then, situated at the Lakeside Caravan Site in Bishop's Cleeve. Rosemary got pregnant by

Fred in January 1970, and at the end of March they went to collect Charmaine from her foster parents' in Tewkesbury. They spent short spells – Fred, Rosemary, Anna Marie, and Charmaine – living in Cheltenham and at 10 Midland Road in Gloucester. But before long they moved up the street, to the ground-floor flat at number 25. Charmaine started at St John's School in Gloucester on 3 September 1970.

In October, Rosemary gave birth to her first daughter, Heather. The following March, Charmaine was taken to Gloucester Royal Hospital with a hurt ankle, but she was not kept in. Charmaine was eight years old. She had long black hair and dark eyes. She still had some baby teeth, and some gaps at the front. She was four and a half feet tall. After the visit to the hospital, there were no further records of Charmaine Carol Mary West. Her remains were eventually discovered under the kitchen floor at 25 Midland Road. They were found at nine thirty in the morning, on 5 May 1994.

Fred married Rosemary Letts early in 1972. She was eighteen. On the marriage certificate Fred described himself as a bachelor. They rented a new house that year, from the same landlord who owned the property at Midland Road, Mr Zygmund. It was just over the other side of the Spa Park – 25 Cromwell Street. Fred worked for a while in places like the Gloucester Wagon Works, then at Dowmac, the concrete works. But he increasingly earned his living as a builder, and he started converting the house at Cromwell Street almost as soon as they moved into it.

The rooms at the top of the house were turned into bedsits and they were soon known to be among the cheapest in Gloucester. All through the seventies, and well into the eighties, young men and women would come and go from the cheap rooms at 25 Cromwell Street. Fred would often ask the young girls who'd been around for a while if they wanted to stay, stay there for good, and work as a nanny. The house grew in size, and so did the family, over the next two decades. Gloucester changed a lot during that period too. The city grew in numbers; a lot of those coming to live there during those years were New Commonwealth immigrants. There was too little work, and most of the incomers were living in areas of cheap housing and privately rented bed-sit accommodation. Cromwell Street, increasingly, was at the centre of one such area. Nearly all the houses had bedsitters in them, though some, like number 25, were not keen to put up immigrants and their families. The local housing department started giving out a list of bedsits in the late seventies. Number 25 was on the list. Fred also put an advert in the Gloucester *Citizen*.

Linda Gough had shoulder-length fair hair, and she often wore oval glasses. She was quite into fashion, and she would do herself up, always buying loads of jewellery from Woolworths. She was born in Gloucester on 1 May 1953, the eldest of three. Linda first went to Linden Road School, then she went to the Longford School for kids with learning difficulties. She spent a little while at a private girls' school in Midland Road after that, which was run by a couple of elderly spinsters. She had no academic qualifications, and she left school when she was sixteen. At that time, she went to work as a seamstress at the Co-op in Gloucester, at the corner of Barton Street. June Gough, Linda's mother, says that she and her husband John were slightly on top of Linda around that time. They thought she was being quite childish, and naïve, and they didn't like the boy she was hanging around with. He was scruffy, and they wanted her to get rid of him.

One lunchtime, on or around 19 April 1973, Linda came home early from work and left a note. It said *Dear Mum and Dad, Please don't worry about me I've got a flat and I'll come and see you sometime. Love Linda.* They never saw her again. They wrote to the DHSS, contacted the Salvation Army, and got their neighbour, a PC Stevens, to look into it. She was never officially registered as a misper. Her remains were discovered under the bathroom floor at 25 Cromwell Street on 10 March 1994.

Carol Anne Cooper was born at the Luton and Dunstable Maternity Hospital on 10 April 1958. Her parents had only been married a year, and the family went to live in Leighton Buzzard soon after the baby was born. In 1962, the parents separated, and Carol Anne went to live with her mother, but her mother died in 1966. Carol Anne then went to live with her father, Colin Cooper, who by that time had married somebody else. They lived on Laxton Avenue, in Worcester. But things weren't working out; Carol Anne couldn't get on with them, and she was eventually taken to the Pines Children's Home in Worcester. She was fond of Indian ink, and would give herself tattoos using a sewing needle. She was always running away from the home. She would get on buses, and try to get away to another life. Late in 1973 she ran off again. But this time she wasn't found. The Pines Home reported her missing to the police. There was a newspaper campaign, and her picture appeared on TV as a missing person. No one came forward.

Lucy Partington wore her hair long, in the style of 1973, and she looked at the world through a pair of gold-rimmed spectacles. She was born on 4 March 1952. Lucy had gone to school in Cheltenham, before finishing at Pates' Grammar School. She was always doing things. At Pates', she worked on the school newspaper and was one for getting the rest of them up and going. Ruth Elisabeth Owen worked on the school rag alongside her. Ruth thought Lucy was good fun; she liked her a lot. They'd sometimes go for walks together across Pitville Park. Helen Render was another friend of Lucy's at Pates'. Lucy had always been kind to her. Helen had been handicapped since birth. She and Lucy had met and become friends in the History Group. They stayed friends, even after school.

In October 1970 Lucy went to the University of Exeter to study medieval English. She was a good student, and a faithful friend, and she continued to work well through 1972 and '73. During the Michaelmas term of 1973, and after no little deliberation, she was received into the Catholic Church. Her mother Margaret lived outside Cheltenham, in the village of Gretton. She was divorced from Lucy's father by then; he had remarried. It was to her mother's that Lucy came for Christmas 1973, arriving at the house on 20 December. Whenever she was down that way, in Cheltenham, she'd always spend as much time with her old friend Helen as she could. Helen says her house was like a second home to Lucy. They still kept their old school nicknames: Helen called her pal Loose-the-Juice. The two girls got together on the 22nd and the 23rd, and on Christmas Eve itself. Helen was mostly confined in a wheelchair, and she wasn't feeling well at that time, so Lucy seemed to make a special effort for her. On the evening of the 27th, Lucy and her brother David came into Cheltenham together. He went off to see a friend, and she went over to Helen's. They sat watching TV most of the evening, an old movie or something. They talked abut the future; they were both interested in history and art. They always had been. Lucy decided to get some notepaper and write to the Courtauld Institute in London, to see if she might be considered for a place. She didn't think there'd be much chance, but she wrote the letter all the same. At ten fifteen she got her things together, and said her goodbyes to Helen. She was going for the last bus out to Gretton, and was planning to post the letter to the Courtauld on the way. There was a post-box right beside the bus stop, which was just a little up the road, about three minutes' walk away, at the corner of Albermarle Gate and Cleveland Drive. She left with the letter in her hand. That was it.

In 1974 Therese Siegenthaler was living in Deptford, South London. She was born in Switzerland on 27 November 1952, and had come to Britain to study sociology at Middlesex Polytechnic. She spoke very good English, and was well known for her confidence and energy, as well as her interest in political things. She had made plans to go to Ireland during the Easter holiday, 1974. She was going over there to visit a priest in Roscommon who shared her interest in South Africa. She went to a party in North London on the evening of 15 April. She stayed the night there, and in the morning she went back to Deptford to get her stuff for Ireland. She set off for Holyhead that afternoon, and she was due back in London on 23 April, to go to the theatre. She never reached Ireland. She was reported missing to the Metropolitan Police on 26 April. Her family contacted Interpol, who got involved in the search for Therese. She was a registered missing person, until 5 March 1994.

Among the missing, you'll sometimes find girls who were always somehow out of sight, even when they were not. Very few people actually knew Shirley Hubbard, and there are even fewer who remember her now. She was born on 26 June 1959 in Worcester, to Glenys Lloyd and Owen John Owen. But her

231

parents split up when she was two. She was taken into care at that age, and was fostered by a Mr and Mrs Hubbard when she was six. They lived in Droitwich – just over six miles outside Worcester. She ran away from there in October 1974. Her disappearance was reported and she was found camping in a field just a mile or so away. The following month, aged fifteen and a half, she went off to do some prearranged work experience at Debenhams in Worcester. There was a boy who worked at a shop in Worcester High Street, Daniel Davies. She'd met him, and went over to his house for her tea. They went to the pictures that night. On the way out, they made an arrangement to get together again the next day, but she didn't turn up. He never heard from her again, and neither did any of the few who had known her.

Juanita Mott lived with her older sister, Georgina, and the younger one, Belinda, at a house in the Coney Hill area of Gloucester. Juanita had her own ideas – she rebelled against everything. When her parents split up she tried to live with her mother's friend Jennifer Baldwin and her family. But that didn't work so well. She left school in 1972, when she was fifteen, and went to live at a number of bedsits in and around Gloucester. She met a guy called Timothy Davies, and she lived with him for a while at a flat in Stroud Road. She left him early in 1975 to go and live at a flat in Cromwell Street. But this wasn't very good either. She went back to live at Jennifer Baldwin's bungalow in Newent in the spring. Mrs Baldwin was about to get married; she had a large group of children and Juanita agreed to look after them on the wedding day. Juanita went out the night before the wedding, but she never returned.

Some time after the summer of 1975, Fred West infilled the

floor of his cellar with concrete. He spread the cement over the whole area, as much as a foot thick, and painted it. He then turned the area into a bedroom for his ever-expanding family of young children.

Shirley Anne Robinson was pregnant when she went missing. Everybody says she was really cheerful; she just wanted to have fun. She was born on 8 October 1959 in Rutland; her parents were at that time living at HMS *Cottersmore*. They split up in 1962. It was Shirley's father who looked after her at first. She was difficult, Shirley, and in 1974 she went to stay with her mother in Hartlepool. But her mother couldn't cope either, and she was quickly taken into care by Bristol social services. In 1975 she was receiving special care at a residential school. She did a lot of work experience – preparing for life outside. Early in 1977 she went to work as a nanny in Chipping Sodbury. She registered at a health centre soon after, giving her address as 25 Cromwell Street. She visited the centre in October 1977 and had a pregnancy test. She was six weeks.

Linda Greening lived at the time in 24 Cromwell Street, right across from where Shirley was staying. She remembers that it was hot, that summer of 1977. They all used to go round to the corner shop in Wellington Street and buy Mr Men ice-lollies. On 10 April 1978 the Gloucester Sickness Benefit Office got a claim from Shirley Anne Robinson. She was pregnant, and was claiming supplementary benefit. John Buckley, her GP at the health centre, saw her on 2 May. He spoke to her about extra benefits she might have been entitled to from the DHSS, as it was then. Her baby was due sometime in June. Shirley's best friend at the time was Liz Brewer, who lived on the floor above her at the house. On 9 May the two of them went into town. They went to Woolworths, and got their pictures taken together in one of those Photo-Me booths. Liz wrote the date on the back of the photostrip. Shirley was gone the next day.

EVERY TIME I went to Gloucester there was something wrong with the weather. It poured or it hailed. It always did, and it made the place seem darker than it is; it made the story seem as sad as it was. The clouds were black-bottomed as I walked up the High Street to meet Liz Brewer. It was a Saturday afternoon, and it had that feeling – I could recall such days stuck in the house as a kid, away from the heathen weather, filling in picture books with scuzzy felt-tips. Our living-room, from the carpets up, would be a veritable colosseum of boredom. There'd be racing on *Grandstand*, or an old film on BBC2. It would always be Robin Hood or someone else filling the screen, looking much more colourful than it was right to be on a day like that.

The High Street wasn't very long. I found the house, but stepped into the corner shop next door to buy some cigarettes before going in. As I stood there, in front of the counter, there was a flash of lightning outside, then a rumble. It's always a bit dramatic, that. The woman behind the counter was going on as if this, indeed, was the end of the end. Thunder and lightning often have that effect, making you feel as if you're being spoken to from somewhere above; it's all a bit afflicting, and terrible. Then the rain came on and the woman went back to inserting the till roll. But that day was the first time I was ever embarrassed by the weather. I waited a minute or so for it to go away, for it to stop banging and cursing, before I went next door and knocked on the door.

Liz Brewer was curling a young girl's hair when I came in.

She was styling it to be just like her own: wavy all round the sides and flat at the crown. But the girl's hair was shorter and brown in colour; Liz's was pure blonde. They were grouped around the mirror. Liz smiled over. There was a word-processor glowing in the other corner, the screen covered in text. The house belonged to the father of the girl in the hairdressing chair. He was Liz's former brother-in-law. He was helping her to write an account of the part of her life spent at 25 Cromwell Street. He was a mechanic, but he'd always wanted to try his hand at writing. He was telling me this, and fixing coffee, as the girls continued to do their thing at the mirror. There were pictures of dolphins and killer whales on the walls, and I spotted, hanging above them, something I was to see again in this county: framed City & Guilds certificates.

Liz was brought up in St Mark's Street in Gloucester. She rowed with her mum from a fairly early age and she went, when she was able, to live in the Toughley area. She was seventeen when she caught sight of an advertisement in the *Citizen*, offering bedsit accommodation for seven pounds a week. It was a good deal, and tenants were allowed to use the washing machine and all that stuff at no extra cost. She said that Shirley Anne Robinson was quite lonely when she met her. A girl called Gloria Langdon was living there at the same time; so was Anna Maria West, and all the children were in a bedroom in the basement. Liz got a job in Tracey's disco – now Crackers – and she felt like she was having the time of her life.

She sat down beside me on the sofa. Before we began to talk properly, she warned me that she was writing something herself, with Brian, and that she wanted to keep things back for it. She wanted to tell the story of what life had been like then, in that house. I said that was fine and proper. I wasn't expecting to go into the house much at all. I was doing something else, I said, something about missing persons and their missing stories. She said that was fine: she'd help me where she could. I asked her about the last day she saw Shirley.

'We got our picture taken in Woolworths,' she said, 'and just after that, we came back to the house. I went out to work, leaving Shirley in my room. That was the last time I saw her.' She then said she had often wondered about her over the years. She'd see people in the street who looked just like her and she'd think, I wonder what happened to her. She'd wonder if Shirley'd had a boy. She said that Fred had the gift of the gab, and he would talk sometimes about his past life. He would talk about his ex-wife Rena who now lived up in Glasgow. He said once that he'd had a son in Glasgow, a boy, Stephen, who'd been run over with an ice-cream van. He was always talking about Glasgow to Ped, Liz's then boyfriend, who came from Glasgow. Ped (Peter) was born in Duke Street Hospital. Fred would boast about sex, and tell of how he'd once had it in the middle of Celtic Park.

Liz got pregnant when she was living in Cromwell Street; Ped was the father. She met Fred on the stairs one day and he stopped her. He said that when he was living in Glasgow he'd become experienced in 'medical matters'. He paused. He then said that if she needed any help, what with this pregnancy and everything, then he would help her. It would be their little secret. She said no, and the boy she gave birth to in the house learnt to walk going up and down the same set of stairs. He is now fifteen.

At the point where Liz told me this, Brian's daughter, an early teenager, who was now sitting across from us wearing a giant pair of furry slippers, broke in. She looked at me. 'Do you think missing people could get taken off by aliens?' she asked.

'I guess so. Or maybe,' I said.

'Yes,' she continued, 'I saw a film about that recently. I think it's true.'

Liz sipped at her coffee and brushed back her hair with an open hand. 'But you know something,' she said; 'I would say that some of my years in Cromwell Street were among the happiest of my life. The stuff that's come out has wasted those years. People have said, "How could you live there?" but, you know, if you were someone who'd been on the road, someone who was a bit lost, it could be like a security. Many of us wanted to belong to this, an extended family.'

But it could have been . . . what if . . .

'It sends shivers down me,' she said. 'I remember seeing Alison Chambers sitting in the front room once. And Belinda Mott – Juanita's sister – she used to come round to the house now and then, and that was well after Juanita had gone missing.' Liz said that, despite everything, some good things had come out of all this. 'I've met a girl who lived there for a while, Bev, she works in a bar in Warwickshire now. I was worried about her. And another girl who I used to work with in Tracey's – Karen, I think her name is – she came from Australia and used to stay for summer holidays. It was a great relief to find out she is OK. God knows abut the other girls.' Liz tried to say other things as well, and sometimes her eyes wandered into open space. She'd look into the distance after she said something, quite distracted, as if there were some things you just couldn't discuss. I sat in a taxi with a similar look on myself. The driver spoke of the weather, and I sat nodding, thinking the weather was just embarrassing.

*

1979 FELT LIKE an ending. Nobody really knew what the eighties would be like, and Britain was full of noise that year, full of plots for the future, and talk of a brand-new Britain. Alison Chambers was sixteen, and nice-looking. She never had any money, but she'd spend a lot of time on herself, and take care of the clothes she happened to pick up. She had lived in a children's home in Swansea, but in 1979 she moved to the Jordansbrook Home in Gloucester. Alison struck up a friendship there with a girl round about her own age called Sharon Compton. Sharon was good for a laugh; she and Alison would share make-up and music with each other. Alison got a place on a Youth Training Scheme, working as a junior in a solicitor's office. The two friends would often walk through the parade of shops in the centre of Gloucester and they met a girl here – her middle name was 'Anne' or something. Sharon remembered that the girl had an Indian-ink tattoo on her arm. It said *Kevin*, with a row of dots under the name. The girl took them to a house in Cromwell Street.

Sharon was working then at a place called the Huddlecourt Garden Hotel. Like Alison, though, she hadn't moved out to a flat or anything; she still lived at Jordansbrook. After a while, she wouldn't see Alison as much, as she always seemed to be out. Alison had become obsessed with going to live on a farm, a place outside Tewkesbury, where someone she met said she could go and live, and ride horses, and write poetry. Sharon remembers seeing Alison with a bit of headed notepaper that was supposed to have come from this farm. It said *Tulip*, or *Tew Valley*, at the top. Alison would sit dreaming over it, drawing ivy all the way up the sides. She once showed her friend a key ring with two keys on it. She smiled: they were hers.

Sometime in September 1979 Alison's mother got a hand-written letter from her daughter. The envelope had a Northamptonshire postal mark. In the note, Alison said that she was living with a really nice homely family. One of the girls treated her just like a big sister. Alison looked after the children and did housework. That was just about all it said. Around then, she gave up her place in the solicitor's office, and she left Jordansbrook one afternoon with a rucksack. The Home was used to it; girls of Alison's age often made off, desperate for a life of their own, and there was little the carers could do about it. She walked off, and no one heard anything else about her. Her documentary life stopped; none of her personal identification numbers or documents was used again. There came the time when people stopped asking themselves where she'd gone. She just wasn't to be seen.

As we watch each of those girls walk away towards nothingness, towards a local grave that was long unknown, we might continue to wonder about their lives. Like Rena Costello and Anne McFall, many of them were no strangers to trouble; and yet, again like the Glasgow girls, they never knew trouble that could take you away for ever. Most of them had just wanted a nice house to live in. Westworld got to them. It was a world serially turning, one ever ready to draw people towards – and over – the brink of disaster and evil. It was a world where some terrifying, and terrifyingly human, magnetism could bring unsuspecting ones to itself. It was a domestic world, but one hard to see. The Glasgow women seem to have been the beginning of this particular series of terrible ends, and we are left to consider the losing of their lives, and the losing of many others after them, and perhaps to see that they were all lost too easily.

Most of the mispers of Gloucester had spent more time on

this earth unseeable than seen. That is their tragedy. Their communities had no way of really missing them; as with many of the missing, we failed to see that they couldn't be seen, and that is always a tragedy too. Like the young girl I left sleeping so soundly in the shelter at Leicester Square, the girls didn't expect the harm that was coming, and neither could we. In many respects they could have been any girl, cut off from the protective life. They could also have been any girl, not so cut off; they could be girls free of damage and neglect too, girls who wrote notes to the Courtauld that never got sent. They all come from somewhere; the passage to nowhere never looked so easy.

I WAS STAYING overnight, and I got the address of a place in Gloucester's Heathville Road. It just said B&B in white paint on a piece of card by the road. The guy who opened the door had a cracker of a black eye. He brought me into the basement flat, which I assumed was his. It was stale; a spongy brown sofa lay folded down in front of the TV; there was a wee pyramid of screwed-up socks in the corner. He dug around for keys while I stood behind the sofa, waiting for him. It wasn't that late, but I felt exhausted, and thought I could just write a few notes and read the paper, and then go to sleep all the way through to the morning. The black eye led me out of the door and up a broken stairwell. Everything was falling apart. We passed a payphone in the hall. There was a sign above which said: *This should not be used to make calls or receive calls before 7 p.m.*

The place was more like a shelter than a commercial hotel. Everyone there was single, nearly all of them were young girls with babies, and all were homeless and on benefit. The DSS sent people there all the time. A couple of girls sat in the communal kitchen with mugs of tea. They were giggling and slagging each other off, and waiting the little while still left before they could use the phone. I went up to the top floor. The room was tiny, with pink walls. A chest of drawers stood next to the bed, with one of the drawers missing. There was a tallboy next to that painted with gloss. There were pipes hanging out of the wall, travelling round, and disappearing outside or to another floor. The bulb was quite naked. I could see all the way outside as I lay on the bed. I sat on it with my head against the board, looking out. This was just another place, I thought, although you couldn't say it felt like a good one. It felt miles away from decency and hope, but I knew some of that feeling was just from feeling so tired.

The sky was red at the top. It looked, that streaked bit of air, like a detail from another place and time. I remembered skies like that. I used to see one just like it, spread above the trees at the beginning of Whitehurst Park in Ayrshire. I could see the exact colour in my memory. I could see it from the bed there too. It looked in every way as burning bright as it had then, from the swing-park at the top of Pennyburn. I would go back there soon, and go to Glasgow, to see the houses of my grandparents. There would be different lights on in those houses this evening, different lights, in those houses that remained.

ACKNOWLEDGEMENTS

MANY PEOPLE HELPED ME to make this book. In Glasgow, in Ayrshire, in Gloucester and in London, people opened up to me about their lives and losses. It wasn't easy for any of them, and their trust helped me to document things as I'd set out to do. A fair number of individuals, and their families, believed in this search for the missing – in the search for one's own – and I wouldn't have got very far without them.

I also owe thanks to the many staff who helped me. Those in the Glasgow Room of the Mitchell Library, the Scottish Record Office, New Register House in Edinburgh, Strathclyde Regional Archive, the British Library, Metropolitan Police, North Ayrshire Museum, Irvine Burns Club, Strathclyde Police, National Missing Persons Helpline, the Lord Chancellor's Department, Camden Social Services, Centrepoint: Off the Street, City of London Coroner's Court, and the People's Palace.

Nancy O'Hagan, my mother, Gerald O'Hagan, my father,

and my eldest brother, Michael, all answered questions and did what they could for me. They often talked without quite knowing why I asked, and I hope they know how much their support meant to me.

I researched and wrote this book whilst working at the *London Review of Books*. To my former colleagues there: many thanks. Mary-Kay Wilmers always looked out for me; I hope not to have let her down.

There are many people who were good with cars and advice – or who were just good, in ways that made a difference. Thanks to Jane Swan, Jeannie Gorman, John Lanchester, Darryl Pinckney, Pete McGinlay, Karl Miller, Sophie Woodforde, Kevin McMunigal, Keith Martin, Bill McArthur, Isa McNeil, Patricia Beer, John Gunion, Alison Menzies, Audrey Gillan, Nadya Kooznetzoff, Edward Manson, Sam Frears, Fiona Carpenter, Dr R. Chambers, Suzanne Dean, Barbara Reid, Francesca Lepper, Nicholas Blake, and Derek Johns.

My editor, Jonathan Riley, and my publisher, Peter Straus, are gentlemen. Their loyalty and good humour made everything easier.

To all these people, with their sometimes spectacular acts of kindness, I offer a ton of thanks. Needless to say, any spectacular mistakes I claim for myself.

Andrew O'Hagan
London, July 1995